WASSERSTROM GP94

5⁹⁵

D0759682

TO TOUCH
THE DIVINE

A Jewish Mysticism Primer

Published by
MERKOS L'INYONEI CHINUCH, Inc.
770 Eastern Parkway
Brooklyn, N.Y. 11213

TO TOUCH THE DIVINE
(A Jewish Mysticism Primer)

Copyright © 1989
MERKOS L'INYONEI CHINUCH
770 Eastern Parkway, Brooklyn, N. Y. 11213
Tel. (718) 774-4000
Printed in the U.S.A.
5749 • 1989

Library of Congress Cataloging-in-Publication Data

To touch the divine.

Papers delivered at the International Symposium
on Jewish Mysticism, held in London in 1981.
Includes index.
1. Mysticism--Judaism--Congresses. 2. Judaism--Congresses.
I. Rader, Benzion. II. Rader, Hilda. III. International Symposium
on Jewish Mysticism (1981) London, England.
BM723.T6   1989   296.8'33
ISBN 0-8266-0494-3
Library of Congress Catalog Card No. 89-15349

EMPIRE PRESS
550 EMPIRE BLVD. • BROOKLYN, N.Y. • (718) 756-1473
FAX (718) 604-7633

Table of Contents

To *contemplate, and meditate*
    Upon His great Design,

To sigh in awe, and do naught else,
    Does not one's soul refine.

To keep His Law, His Statutes all
    To Him one's self resign,

Is to soar above this mundane world;
    To touch the Divine.

B.R.

RABBI MENACHEM M. SCHNEERSON
Lubavitch
770 Eastern Parkway
Brooklyn. N. Y. 11213

493-9250

מנחם מענדל שניאורסאהן
ליובאוויטש

770 איסטערן פּאַרקוויי
ברוקלין, נ. י.

By the Grace of G-d
10th of Nissan, 5741
Brooklyn, N.Y.

To all Participants in the
International Symposium on
Jewish Mysticism
Sponsored by the Lubavitch Foundation
London, England.

Greeting and Blessing:

I was pleased to be informed of the forthcoming Symposium on Jewish Mysticism, and extend prayerful wishes for its success. And success, or rather *hatzlachah* in its true Jewish concept, is rooted in the Torah, which insists on the primacy of action — "the essential thing is the deed."

Mysticism, in general, has a variety of connotations, but Jewish mysticism must necessarily be defined in terms of specific topics that have to do with the *nistar* of Torah — one of the two primary facets of the Torah: *nigleh* and *nistar*, the revealed and the hidden. Needless to say, there can be no dichotomy between the two, because it is One Torah, given by One G-d, to the "one people on earth." According to the *Baal Shem Tov's* interpretation, the words "one people on earth" allude to the mystic nature of the Jewish soul that is endowed with the capacity to reveal the oneness in the multiplicity of earthly things.

Jewish mysticism teaches that the purpose of the soul's descent to earth is to reveal the harmony that is inherent in the created world, beginning with the "small world," namely, man — a creature of *nigleh* and *nistar*, of a body and a soul. Inner personal peace and harmony can be achieved only through the supremacy of the soul over the body, since in the nature and scheme of things, the body can be made to submit to the soul — willingly, and in the case of the true mystic even eagerly; but not *vice versa*.

Jewish mysticism helps to realize the said purpose of the soul by teaching it how to recognize the spirituality of matter, and that in every physical thing, even in the inanimate, there is a "soul," which is the creative force that has created it — a being out of non-being — and continuously keeps from reverting back to its former state of non-existence. It is this "spark" of G-dliness that is the true essence and reality of all things, and this spark is released and revealed when physical matter is used for a sublime purpose or deed in accordance with the Will of the Creator, as, for example, in the performance of a *mitzvah* (*tefillin* made of leather, etc.).

One of the aspects of Chabad is to *reveal* and expound the esoteric aspects of the Torah and *mitzvot* so that they can be comprehended by the three intellectual faculties — *chochmah*, *binah*, *daat*, and reduced to rational categories, down to the actual performance of the *mitzvot*, showing how, in the final analysis, G-d can be "comprehended" better by action (the performance of *mitzvot*) than by meditation, which is one of the cardinal differences between Jewish and non-Jewish mysticism.

As we are about to celebrate *Pesach*, the Festival of our Freedom, we are reminded that *yetziat mitzrayim* (in the sense of *metzarim*, constraints) is a continuous process of Jewish living, gaining an ever-growing measure of true freedom through the everyday experience of Torah and *mitzvot* with emphasis on actual deed.

> With esteem and blessing for a
> *Kosher* and inspiring *Pesach*,
>
> /Signed: Menachem Schneerson/

Foreword

Was it not an extravagant gesture to arrange an International Symposium on Jewish Mysticism at a time when Jewish learning and observance are at such a low ebb? Wouldn't an extension of one or more of the basic learning programs have been more appropriate? How can one speak of *Kabbalah* to men and women, some of whom can barely read the *Alef-Bet*?

These questions are not entirely hypothetical or new; neither are the attitudes they mirror. For they parallel the questions and charges that were levelled against the *Chassidic* movement when it first emerged over 200 years ago.

At that time, too, many who opposed this new force within Judaism did so on the grounds that it was not the time to reveal the "secrets" of the *Torah* to the masses. Yet in the decades that followed, great rabbis and scholars, many initially opposed and antagonistic to the teachings of the *Baal Shem Tov* or to their general revelation, joined a movement that was dedicated to expounding the esoteric truths of Judaism at all levels and to Jews everywhere.

And just as the intervening two-and-a-half centuries have vindicated the actions of the *Baal Shem Tov*, his followers and their successors, so too did the positive response to the almost week-long symposium show how well its organizer, the Lubavitch Foundation of Great Britain, had judged Anglo-Jewry's mood and needs.

What is that mood? What are those needs?

With almost every advance in science and certainly as a result of space exploration, the order that exists within the physical universe becomes more apparent. Nothing is haphazard. And it becomes increasingly difficult for any thinking person to dismiss a metaphysical dimension to the universe.

Yet, paradoxically, within mankind the opposite would seem to apply. There is a growing lack of order. Whether in those areas that have rarely experienced greater affluence or in those which still, to our shame, experience great deprivation, the world would seem to be hurtling towards disaster. Ecologists predict it, conservationists predict it. Pollution of every kind — physical, moral, ethical, spiritual — is having a disastrous effect on standards, values, life and living.

These two realities postulate perplexing problems for each man and woman.

Where does one individual, a tiny speck in time and space, stand in the total scheme of things?

How can one person influence events which are so often beyond his ken?

Is there any purpose in trying to exercise disciplines, the effects of which one doesn't see or understand? Should one even try to avert the impending disaster to which humanity appears condemned or should one live just for the day?

These, and many others of a similar ilk, are real questions. To the Jew or Jewess — the survivalists of the world — they have a particular pertinence. Were all the trials and sufferings of the millenia overcome just to end like this? Or is there a purpose to life contained within our faith, of which we have never been made aware? What part does an apparently meaningless rote of prayer and observance play in that purpose? Many of the answers we seek are contained in Jewish mysticism.

Jewish mysticism is as old as the Jewish people and yet it was not until some 250 years ago that esoteric teachings were generally revealed. And, as is often the case, it took a crisis in Jewish history to bring about this revelation.

The eighteenth century found Jews in Eastern Europe in a state of misery. Decimated by pogroms extending over half a century, ignored to a lesser or greater extent by the Jewish scholars of the time, Jews were experiencing not so much a crisis of faith as a dilemma of despair.

This tide in the history of Judaism was stemmed and turned by the *Baal Shem Tov*. The profound esoteric teachings that he revealed and taught were not in themselves new. Mystic doctrine concerning G-d and the universe were an integral part of the Revelation at Sinai and had since been studied, preserved and transmitted by a select group of saintly scholars in each generation. The *Baal Shem Tov*'s inspired contribution was his revelation of these teachings to the wider world and his ability to show even the simplest Jew the practical application to his own being of those innermost mystic doctrines. He taught them that each Jew was a microcosm of the entire world.

This is not the place to trace the history of Jewish mysticism before and since the *Baal Shem Tov*. It is sufficient to say that the *Baal Shem Tov*'s teachings were later systematized into a philosophy which has stood the test of time and place.

What do these teachings offer to Jews today?

Today we are experiencing many crises.

First, a crisis of identity. Who are we? Looking so like our non-Jewish neighbors, how are we different? Do we have a special contribution to offer to the troubled world in which we live? The evasion of these questions leads to apathy, to alienation and to assimilation.

Then, a crisis of direction. Where do we stand? Where are we going? These questions lead many of our young — and not so young — to search in foreign fields, disciplines and cults for answers that are provided by their natural heritage: a heritage to which, for whatever reason and through whatever cause, they have had little or no access.

A crisis of faith. Although in reality this is often little more than the manifestation of lack of knowledge. How can one believe when one has such sparse knowledge of the tenets of one's faith?

Finally, a crisis of stability. The family unit, the fulcrum on which Jewish existence and survival have always been tenderly balanced, is disintegrating and disappearing. Gaps in ideas and ideals between one generation and another have widened into chasms. Relationships mean little, divorce is rife.

Self-indulgence and self-gratification, all too often packaged as self-fulfillment and self-expression, are today's best-sellers. And indeed, "self" is the common factor in all these crises. It is a conflict of self that begets many of the crises that Jews throughout the world face today.

And it is "self" which Jewish mysticism addresses. For mysticism begins with self and ends with self. Knowledge of self is a means to knowledge of the Creator and also to knowledge of the created universe. For just as physics teaches that energy can never disappear, mysticism teaches the eternality of the Jewish soul. Whether we call it self or ego, it is soul to which we really refer — the human soul acting through the free will given to us.

Jewish mysticism expounded on the human will and human psychology and libido long before Freud introduced these terms into the science of psychoanalysis. It conceives the human body as containing all the natural dispositions inherent in man as a creature of the world. In their pristine state they are not evil but neutral forces which ideally are to serve as the vehicle for the human soul which must act through them.

Man, with his physical and spiritual powers, is a replica of Primordial Man, the first manifestation of the Divine Image, the source of all creation.

Transcendence, immanence, contemplation and meditation, which to so many connote new ideas and disciplines outside Judaism, have at all times been standard terms and concepts in esoteric doctrine.

As the intellectual arm of the *Baal Shem Tov*'s teachings, *Chabad*, founded by Rabbi Schneur Zalman of Liadi, the first Chabad-Lubavitch leader, is a philosophy that integrates mystical and rational currents of Jewish thought, blending them into one cohesive religious system. It is a philosophy that rejects the idea that simple faith is all that is required in man's relationship to G-d. For it insists that the mystical union of man and G-d can best be achieved through intellectual comprehension.

The Lubavitch Foundation of Great Britain has regularly invited eminent thinkers and scholars to speak and lecture on mysticism. It was, however, considered that the spiritual darkness that we now experience requires a more intensive light.

Hence the International Symposium on Jewish Mysticism.

The varied and various sessions ranged from a small weekend seminar with its talks, discussions and tutorials, and a one-day seminar, both at the Oxford Centre for Management Studies; a student brunch at Hillel House, London; to large public meetings in London, Manchester, Leeds and Glasgow, culminating in a "Meeting of Minds" at the Royal Institution, London. Over 1,500 men and women of all ages and from all walks of life — a wide cross section of Anglo-Jewry — attended one or more of the sessions and met a "team" that conveyed lofty, abstract thoughts in practical, relevant terms. The "team" — five scholars of international repute; men of learning and faith — demonstrated that Jewish mysticism was not just an academic subject, but an intrinsic component of their total Jewish experience.

A letter from the Lubavitcher Rebbe had set the tone of the Symposium. In a few succinct and measured paragraphs, the Rebbe stated the essential difference between Jewish and non-Jewish mysticism: how "G-d can be 'comprehended' better by action than by meditation" and how Jewish mysticism teaches the soul to recognize the spirituality of matter.

The "team" soon made one aware that the esoteric and exoteric in Judaism were not separate, but two parts of the same whole and that Judaism contained the answers to those dilemmas that caused one to search elsewhere or to give up the search altogether. While their approach to the subject was broad and varied, they combined to show the part the Divine plays in every aspect of our day-to-day life.

This volume cannot recapture the spirit of those few days or the full range of the talks, discussions and interplay of ideas. It cannot portray the many moments of high emotion and quiet humor. It does not set out to do so.

In reproducing some of the papers that were presented,

augmented by a small selection of other material on the same subject, it is hoped that the wider audience this book reaches will find much of interest within it... that some thought or insight will provoke the reader and provide a stimulus to search further within authentic Judaism... so that he or she may be moved to greater observance and reach out in an attempt "to touch the Divine."

Benzion Rader

On Jewish Mysticism

Rabbi Zalman Posner

Mysticism deals with unfamiliar subjects: the stratum underlying the visible, the spiritual beneath the material we perceive. This may involve the universe, it may involve the human soul, it may involve strata of *Torah* interpretation, namely the element called *sod*, the "secret" or esoteric interpretation. Jewish mysticism posits "worlds" other than ours, not off in space, but spiritual rather than physical, "peopled" by spiritual beings commonly referred to as "souls" or "angels." (Because of overtones burdening that last word, we shall frequently use the Hebrew *malach* or *malachim* in plural). This is not some irrelevant flight of fancy or fantasy, but *Torah's* bridge between G-d the Infinite and our world of time and space. Jewish mysticism is not a purely intellectual activity but is fulfilled only when it affects behavior in the most mundane sense.

Chabad expresses its fundamental orientation in the matter of mysticism as it does in every field of *Torah*, *mitzvot*, character development, etc.: it insists on translating every subject into intellectually accessible terms. This means that *Chabad* presents what may be arcane, intangible, amorphous, almost intuitive material in rational terms, as an intellectual discipline subject to all the rigors of such disciplines, including verbalization, communication, clarification, challenge and analysis. The subject attains an objective existence. The mind becomes the instrument for dealing with it, rather than feeling or intuition.

Mysticism has an aura of the esoteric, the mysterious; all rather intimidating. To be sure, this impression may be well-founded but it is not inevitable, for mysticism can be translated into rational terms.

Reality and Symbol

What is reality and what is symbol? The spiritual or the material? *Kabbalah* speaks of counterparts, spiritual and material. Take, for example, *malachim* and animals — an analogy that may seem wildly disparate at first sight, but one that may make sense in a few moments.

Let us first examine the term "angel," commonplace though so distorted in the popular imagination. People apparently tend to picture angels as they appear in religious art; fanciful, totally inappropriate to the subject, hardly to be taken seriously. So the idea of "angels" becomes relegated to other religions that no intelligent person could possibly respect.

We are familiar with physical dimensions, boundaries, shapes and forms; our entire human experience takes place in that context. There are also non-corporeal "bodies," dimensions, limitations. Ideas have dimension, love has its "shape" to distinguish it from other feelings. These dimensions of spirit characterize non-physical "beings" or states, giving them personhood, as it were. Imagine a disembodied, independent being called "awe," for example, or "comprehension," with an existence apart from the person's mind or heart.

Malachim, as *Torah* has it, are personifications of intellect; beings that apprehend G-d "intellectually," conscious of Him in intellectual terms. Or a *malach* may apprehend G-d through love or awe, that emotion being the dimension of its existence. Mind is not feeling, and the intellect-*malach* is different from the emotion-*malach*; love is not awe, and the love-*malach* is not the same as the awe-*malach*.

"Holy, holy, holy," three times declared, is not a rhetorical flourish. "Holy" means apart, inaccessible, transcending. Apprehension of transcendence may be on an infinite number of planes, for we are dealing with the truly infinite. Each declaration of *kadosh* — "holy" — by a *malach* is that *malach's* apprehension of G-d's transcendence, the second higher than the first, the third still higher.

Each *malach*, whatever its character, was endowed with that trait; it was not the product of effort or initiative, or of inward creativity. G-d made each of them with this one particular characteristic; one-dimensional, if you wish. This is its limitation; unbreachable, inviolate. It is programmed to "know" G-d or "fear" Him or "love" Him, or whatever its character may be. Love will express itself in attraction, awe or fear through withdrawal or *bitul*, nullification, and so on. Though each trait may exist on an infinte number of planes, each *malach* is monochromatic.

Now a crucial point: there is no growth among *malachim*. The prophet Zechariah calls them "standing" (in contrast to man who is "progressing" or "walking"). There is no choice, no option, no temptation, no self-indulgence, no weakness — hence no growth. As it was made, so it remains: predictable, preordained, stable. This defines the essence of the *malach*, the spiritual being, the total servant or messenger of G-d — unfailing, perfect. In short, an "angel." Its love of G-d is all-consuming, its awe is absolute, its intellectual apprehension on whatever scale is profound and exalted.

Carrying the *malach*-animal analogy further, we must again define the essence of a *malach*. Not the variable, ancillary characteristics, but that it is endowed and predictable. This, too, is the essence of the animal. As it was created, so it remains. Anticipation is largely fulfilled, potential usually becomes reality. A calf will give milk one day. It won't articulate a Theory of Relativity the next. So *malach* and animal are not all that wildly different.

In a sense, what we have tried to do in these paragraphs is to use the *Chabad* approach. *Chabad* seeks to plumb beyond the visible, the material. What is the essence of *malach* and what is the essence of animal? We find that even if they are not identical, there is sufficient similarity to draw a connection, a parallel, a reality-symbol relationship. And *Chabad* does this in rational terms, so that, after accepting certain premises, the reasoning all falls into place.

Man stands apart from both *malachim* and beasts, though he does share some of each; a "little lower than the angels" and possessing an "animal" soul, as the *Tanya* explains in the very first chapter. Man's essence is sharply different. Man is complex, a composite; the animal and the G-dly, mind and emotion, body and soul, idealistic and indulgent. Which will dominate? He is unpredictable. He chooses, and default is also a choice. He determines all. In absolute terms, his intellect-grasp of G-d and his emotion-grasp are grossly inferior to that of *malachim* (except for a truly majestic soul like *Moshe Rabbenu*). But he has the quality of growing, struggling, overcoming innate weaknesses and handicaps so he can progress, he can develop. He is not preordained, he has an infinite potential. He can create within himself a penetrating mind out of a clod, a sensitive heart from an unfeeling ego. Humanness is the capacity to change and grow. So *Chabad* delves into the essence of man, discovers a spark of infinity there and makes it quite comprehensible.

And now we shall return to our primary subject.

Which is the "real" reality and which the symbol — the physical or the spiritual? Here we have a problem — or fact — of perspective, as *Chassidut* frames it: *daat tachton* and *daat elyon* (knowledge from below and knowledge from Above). From below, meaning our mortal perception, we know that the tangible is real, a "thing," *yesh*, for we can touch that tree and feel it with our hands. The animating, creative word of G-d, "Let there be..." is *ayin* (nothingness). It lies beyond our perception, our understanding, it is beyond description, so it is "nothingness."

But from Above, the creative power is the reality, for without it there can be no existence. So that is the true "thing," existence, while the totally dependent material universe is a chimera, *ayin*, nothingness. Reality and symbol depend on one's premises, where one stands. Boring through tangential properties like physical perceptions to the essence, one realizes that the appearance is on the surface. It is only an effect, has no independent existence, and so the immense physical universe, light-years in magnitude, is only a symbol for a higher reality.

We may venture that Jewish mysticism provides man with another perspective, with insights otherwise possibly denied him. It enables him to examine himself and his world and to perceive what lies beyond perception; a reality that eludes those who cannot penetrate past the obvious. Instead of being overwhelmed by environment and circumstance, man can sense the purpose of his experiences and stand apart and dominate his environment and his world.

Mystical experience

We must differentiate between mysticism and mystical experience. The latter has enjoyed some vogue in the past decade and more, with claims of a special sensitivity and awareness, ecstasy, religious insight, experience and expanded consciousness. Permit some skepticism at this point, and allow a word of clarification and caution.

A mystical experience, an awareness of G-d, from the Jewish perspective, is attained through discipline of self, control of personal desire and gratification. When indulgence is the practice, then one cannot expect a sensitivity to concerns of the soul. Use of hallucinogenics, LSD and other drugs, magical formulas or processes vulgarizes mysticism. Whatever their effects, they don't elevate man.

Why should we dismiss the possible validity of these claims? Devices like drugs are not under man's control. They manipulate man, affect him, change him. He is passive and cannot control results. They are his master and he is a pawn who has abdicated his humanity. We explained earlier that man is man when he makes decisions, when he is autonomous, independent. Conversely, religion becomes effective when man uses his volition to overrule the demands of ego and body, denies the dominance of material and physical power, and dedicates himself to G-d, higher than man. Only then does he approach G-d.

In another context the *Tanya* discusses man tied down below in bondage to his physical desires and futilely attempting to rise higher. It is probably safe to state that a hedonist, and not necessarily in the extreme form, is incapable of having a mystical insight or experience.

Meditation

In his letter, the Rebbe contrasts Jewish and non-Jewish mysticism, particularly citing their respective attitudes to meditation. Non-Jewish mysticism concentrates on meditation and Judaism insists on carrying meditation into intellect and action. This difference is of course characteristic and is not limited to mysticism.

Meditation addresses and involves the mind alone. Not necessarily on the rational intellectual plane, but through intuition, feeling, ecstasy, vision. It is in this way that meditation deals with man's life. *Torah's* approach is different. Scholarship? Of course! Worship with love and awe? No question! But *mitzvot* must be performed or all else is a waste and worse. Meditation ending with meditation is unacceptable.

Judaism does not denigrate this material world. Only here can a *mitzvah* be performed, not in the highest spiritual heavens. And only by fallible man, not by *malachim* crying "*kadosh, kadosh, kadosh.*" Judaism does not advocate escape from the world or its distractions and ills. "When you come into the land..." is almost a refrain of *Torah* introducing *mitzvot*, clearly a goal, a blessing, a fulfillment. Living as an anchorite is not a Jewish ideal.

Meditation involving only mind and heart, and not intended to penetrate further into action and the physical life, may bring its rewards during such meditation. But later and after the exaltation it may bring, man may revert to his previous state, with no apparent effect from his mystical experience. Translating lofty thoughts and emotions into physical deeds is not casual, but deliberate. It is often quite difficult. *Chabad* devotes a remarkable amount of attention to this problem, insisting that the validation of a thought or emotion is its impact on deed.

Even meditation itself, quite apart from its effects, needs examination. We have noted earlier that intellect and mysticism are not identical. Mysticism, in the form of meditation, is also ultimately rather undefinable, unverifiable. The mystic's experience is subjective, not subject to testing or disproving. Who can deny the mystic's claims? Ideas, though, can be objective, examined, disputed, disproven. *Chabad* does not accept mysticism in this form, hence enabling the mystic to test the validity of his own meditation or experience. He can communicate it to others and they can challenge and analyze his words, perhaps rejecting them as self-deception or superficial, or perhaps accepting the mystic as a mentor, learning from him and emulating him.

What is mysticism?

Mysticism is man's attempt to apprehend G-d. By definition, mortal and dimensioned man must have equally limited perception, pathetically inadequate to the task of dealing with the Infinite. In terms of G-d the Infinite, the most exalted attainments of *malachim* and the coarsest physical matter are equally insignificant or even *ayin*, nothingness. In human terms, thought may be a "higher" function than eating, but one is not inherently superior to the other in reference to Infinity.

Creation is possible only for the Infinite, since the gap between physical existence and non-existence is infinite, unbridgeable. G-d's greatness is not expressed in or through *malachim*, the supernal "worlds," but in the creation of this world, the mundane. In parallel, our loftiest thoughts are totally inappropriate and inadequate in apprehending the Infinite. Leather made into *tefillin* is an expression of the Infinite who alone could create them. They are therefore the appropriate vehicle with which man may "grasp" G-d. Meditation by itself cannot achieve this. Meditation in the mind that arouses an emotion like love or reverence for G-d in the heart, however, leads to acts of *mitzvot* performed by the physical body using physical objects (*succah, lulav, matzah, shofar, mezuzah, kashrut, Shabbat, tallit, tzitzit, tzedakah,*) and creates a point of contact between man and G-d that nothing else can achieve.

This is a redaction of a paper delivered by Rabbi Posner to the International Symposium on Jewish Mysticism. The Rebbe's letter to which he refers is reprinted in full at the beginning of this book.

Jewish Mysticism:
Just Another Cult?

———————— Rabbi Dr. J. Immanuel Schochet

Mysticism. The word itself mystifies. It excites feelings of awe and anticipation: an indefinable awe and dread in the awareness of forbidding depths beyond the normative reach of man; yet also anticipation of discovering secrets that confound even as they arouse curiosity.

Man is defined as the rational being. To be rational means to think, and to think means to be inquisitive, to search. Our search encompasses questions about our very being — our source of origin and our ultimate destiny; questions about the meaning of life, the purpose of existence.

Oftentimes we embrace quick answers so that our search may come to rest in some certitude. Yet again and again our certainties are shaken. Some try to escape by denying their doubts. They submerge themselves in social and professional ambitions and identities. Yet moments of spontaneous reflection recur. Thoughts touching issues that transcend the here-and-now force themselves upon us again and again.

Every so often we snatch a glimpse of that transcendence. It may come in a state of contemplation. It may come from a deeply touching experience: from an experience of consummate love, from a perception of the immensity of nature, from being transported to ecstasy by music or poetry, or from so many other experiences that penetrate the very core of our being.

Such glimpses are part of what we call mystical experiences. They are not restricted to a select circle of initiates to the esoteric sciences, nor to those who have withdrawn from the mundane. The mystical experience, in the wide sense of the term, is an integral part of the human experience. It is native to all people, without distinction of race or creed. With some more, with others less — yet, universal.

The universality of mysticism is both fascinating and problematic. It has made mysticism the subject of academic study and scientific research — to be analyzed, classified and categorized by professionals in the fields of theology, philosophy and psychology. For the mark of mysticism is not only the intense feeling of the mystical experience, but also, and more so, its effects.

Nothing is closer to man than an actual experience. The more gripping — the more real it is to him. Thus it is not surprising that experience causes man to draw practical conclusions affecting his philosophical perspective and judgments.

Obviously, these conclusions are relative to the experience, to the degree of its intensity and its perceived relevance. They are also relative to the individual's mind and emotions. In other words, these conclusions are highly subjective. They may differ drastically one from the other, even contradicting one another. They are influenced by many varying factors: personal background, previous commitments or inclinations; they are colored by mental and psychological conditioning.

The mystical experience

This leads to our basic problem: how authentic is the experience? How reliable are the "vibrations" and how valid are the conclusions? How and where do we draw the line between the authentic and the spurious, between the reliable and the deceptive, the true and the imagined, the valid and the specious?

William James, a well-known philosopher and psychologist, summarized four distinguishing marks of the mystical experience:

(a) Ineffability: it defies expression. That is, no adequate report of its content can be given in words. Its quality must be experienced directly: mystical states are more states of feeling than states of intellect.

(b) Noetic quality: the mystical experience appears to the subject as a state of knowledge, an insight into the depths of truth that are unplumbed by the discursive intellect. It is an illumination, indeed a "revelation," full of significance and importance, inarticulate though it remains.

(c) Transiency: it cannot be sustained for long.

(d) Passivity: it "hits" the subject, grasping and holding him like a power beyond him, beyond his control, as if his own will is in abeyance. To be sure, the experience can be induced by voluntary operations as, for example, fixing attention (meditation), bodily performances (e.g., yoga exercises), or intoxicants (alcohol, drugs) that will stimulate the mystical consciousness. Certain aspects of nature may awaken mystical moods. Nonetheless, in the actual experience of the "event," for the "contents" of the experience, the subject is in effect passive.

The most powerful aspect of the mystical experience is clearly the innate feeling that everything is charged with meaning. The subject feels surrounded by "truths" which he is as yet unable to grasp, but they arouse indescribable awe. He is filled with cosmic consciousness, a consciousness of the life and order of the universe. He senses an intellectual enlightenment that leads him to new planes of existence. There is moral exaltation, an indescribable feeling of elation, a quickening of the moral sense — as striking and more important than the enhanced power of the intellect.

Moreover, mystical states, when developed, are usually authoritative for the individual who experiences them; he "has been there" and just "knows."

Here lies both the fascination and the problem, the beauty and the fundamental weakness of mysticism and mystical experiences.

The dilemma: conservatism v. anarchy

Many have already observed that mysticism may move man into various and varying directions: some to conservatism, others to revolution; some to deeper commitments, others to anarchy and nihilism.

For some the experience is a rediscovery of self, enhancing and reinforcing their personal, social or religious identity by lending it deeper meaning, new dimensions. Others again are led to a radical reinterpretation of their philosophical or religious systems, often to an allegorical spiritualization of the external forms and dictates of their tradition. For many it is the conscious or subconscious excuse for a self-indulgent anti-nomianism in which the experience, the personal "turn-on," is the standard and the goal. It does not matter to them whether the experience is a striking flash of intuition from without, or whether it is induced from within by the mechanical means of auto-suggestion, meditation or drugs.

An historical review of mystics and mystical schools, in the East and in the West, within our Jewish tradition and outside of it, readily offers evidence of these trends.

We are familiar with giants of the spirit who were intoxicated by their insights and experiences to a renunciation of the self. They were moved to forgo all pursuits of the ego and submerged themselves in the ultimate reality of omnipresent Divinity to become a vehicle for the Will of G-d.

We know also of movements and individuals who intoxicated themselves to reach altered states of consciousness for their self-indulgence, and used their illusions to justify excesses of all sorts.

This polarity is reflected in the very nature of mysticism. For mysticism is by definition monistic and pantheistic. There are, though, two kinds of pantheism:

(a) There is a physiomonistic pantheism which identifies the world, the physical realm, the here-and-now, as the sole reality. The "I, man, world, nature" that is the centre of all — indeed, is all. Good and evil, therefore, are not distinguishable in any absolute sense; they are but in the eye of the beholder.

(b) There is a theomonistic pantheism which recognizes G-d alone as the ultimate reality: "there is nought but He alone." "I, man, world, nature" — these have no reality of their own and exist solely by virtue of the Creator's Will. This is not simply pantheism, but panentheism: G-d is in all; all is in G-d; G-d is all. The world is not a place that contains Him, but He contains the world. His Will, therefore, is the criterion for right and wrong, good and evil. There are absolute values.

This brings us back to our problem: How and where do we draw the line between authenticity and self-delusion? Are there objective standards to serve as guidelines, or must we find our own way in a chaotic jungle of subjective feelings and relative insights? Are mystical schools just different fads or forms of cults — some of which appear acceptable because (generally speaking) they conform to basic social and philosophical standards, while others are rejected because they contravene conventional norms?

As for Jewish mysticism: is it just one other school, just one more facet, in the wide spectrum of mysticism? Is it distinguished from all others merely by its particular religious label, but otherwise essentially the same?

Before trying to answer these questions we must first define the term "cult," expecially in its presently negative connotation of "extravagant and faddish attachment to a person or system of worship or ritual."

What is a cult?

I would define "cult" as any form of faith or belief that is based on an unfounded commitment: a "blind belief," a "blind leap of faith." To be sure, the believer may be altogether sincere. The doctrines or teachings espoused may appear altogether noble. The objectives may seem idealistic and commendable. Nonetheless, if the commitment is based on purely personal feelings and emotions, if it is devoid of any rational foundation and lacks valid "reasons for the belief" (be they historical or philosophical), then we have no choice but to condemn it as a cult.

This definition applies to any form of theological or

philosophical system that is charged with practical consequences; i.e., that would commit its adherents to adopt a distinct way of life and practices.

To determine who would fall into this category one may simply ask: "Why do you follow or accept your belief?"

If the answer contains:

(i) a reason that is more or less defensible from a logical point of view; or

(ii) a reason (or form of reasoning) that the proponent would consider or respect when presented to him in defense of a view differing from (or opposing) his own, then he has shown fair justification for himself.

To be sure, in the latter case he need not necessarily accept the conclusions derived from the other's premises. He may have equally good or better reasons to move into an altogether different direction; but he can at least understand and appreciate the other position — "it does make some sense."

If, however, the premises and conclusions can be shown to be blatantly untrue or invalid; if the reasoning is inconsistent and logically untenable; if the proponent would not accept his own kind of "reasoning" and "proof" when offered by another to justify a radically different or opposite approach, and just stubbornly proclaims: "Just believe! Just accept!" — then he is shown to be self-serving, senseless, acting out of ignorance and/or pure emotionalism. He is not reasoning but rationalizing. He is not in pursuit of truth but of self-justification. He is mentally blind; irrational; in effect — dishonest. His system is no better than the worst he would condemn in others.

This yardstick must be applied to the realm of religion more than anywhere else. For religion is by definition all-encompassing; comprehensive. When speaking of G-d and

religion we are dealing with ultimate truth, the most important thing in life.

We are not talking about transient values, momentary
gains, about "take-it-or-leave-it" propositions. We are not
involved with wagers, taking chances.

To the believer, religion is everything. It relates to his
soul, as opposed to his body. It relates to salvation, as
opposed to comforts. It relates to eternity, as opposed to the
here-and-now. It relates to absolute truth, as opposed to
pragmatism or efficiency.

When it comes to buying a used car, or even the simple
purchase of a common item, we make the effort to investigate, to evaluate, to consider carefully that the article is
worth the surrender of our money. We all know the relative
value of money, and that the loss of even a substantial sum is
not an insurmountable tragedy. Yet we go out of our way to
protect this transient property.

When it comes to obtaining medical advice, even of a
non-vital nature, we make the effort to investigate, to evaluate, to consider carefully, that the doctor is a reliable and
conscientious authority. In more serious cases, as for an
operation — even when there are no life-threatening consequences — we go out of our way to obtain a second opinion,
preferably the opinion of specialists in the field.

Anyone in his right mind goes out of his way to protect
his physical well-being and comfort, and to insure his
worldly property and possessions — notwithstanding the
fact that these are but transient, here-and-now, and can be
protected only up to a certain limit and degree. How much
more so then, must we be careful, critical and investigative
when it comes to matters of religion — matters of spiritual
well-being, salvation, eternity! There is no greater absurdity
than to be more careful with the mundane, with matters

relating to our body and money, than in matters relating to our soul and salvation.

This is the absurdity — indeed insanity and outright self-contradiction — of blind commitments, blind leaps of faith. This is not faith but credulity. This is not "conversion" but seduction. This is not "rebirth" but suicide. It reduces religion to a level far inferior to anything mundane.

A rational person would not buy something just because of its external attractiveness, or because of the charm or oral promises of the salesman. How much less so can or should we accept philosphical or theological premises just because of the emotional magnetism of their external attractiveness and the promised dreams of those soliciting.

We all remember Jim Jones and his Jonestown. We all know horror-stories of youngsters (and elderly) involved with the many other cults of gurus and evangelists. The trouble, though, is that most people recognize the harm and absurdity of those cults because they are so different from our conventional norms — yet fail to ask themselves whether they are really different in principle; whether their own approach to the ultimate issues is different in essence; whether they themselves are not also seduced and brainwashed by emotional magnets, by the allurements of the world or society around them, by values and practices whose meaningfulness and benefits are but relative to a present time and location.

This applies to our approach to G-d and religion in general, and to our personal practices in particular. This applies to the way that many of us seek to mold and shape our religious or ethical principles and practices to our likes and caprices, instead of molding and shaping our likes and caprices to the ultimate dictates and practices of our religion.

An excellent example of this definition and description

of "cult" can be found in a very bizarre source. At the murder trial of the notorious Manson "family" in California, one of the defendants addressed the jury before sentencing: "What I did came from the heart, from love. Whatever comes from the heart and flows out of love cannot be evil. You cannot stand in judgment over me...!"

This emotionalism, this centrality of the heart, this obsession with self — that is the ultimate sign of a cult, the distinctive mark of the crudest of all idolatries: self-worship. True religion deals with the question: "What does G-d require of man?" False religion, a cult, deals with question: "What does man expect from G-d?"

The Uniqueness of Jewish Mysticism

We can now return to the earlier questions.

The line can and must be drawn in the context of an honest, objective and critical self-evaluation. The line can and must be drawn in the context of a frank and open pursuit of truth, regardless of what the consequences may be; without prejudging, without personal bias, without considering what others might think or say. We need no more than the same criteria used in determining our general concept of truth and reality — the same criteria, be they historical or philosophical, no more.

It is here that Jewish mysticism differs radically from all other kinds or schools of mysticism.

Judaism is based on the public Revelation at Sinai, when the *Torah* was given to Israel. The historical event of Sinai attests to the Divine source and nature of the *Torah*, and the *Torah* in turn serves as the exclusive criterion for any subsequent claims and teachings.

Authentic Jewish mysticism is an integral part of *Torah*, and *Torah* determines what is authentic Jewish mysticism.

The general term for Jewish mysticism is *Kabbalah*. *Kabbalah* means tradition. The *Kabbalah* is not a compound of personal insights. It is not a collection of reports of what various Sages and saints had to say on the meaning of life and ultimate values — based on their mystical experiences or visions. It is not a system born in a vacuum.

The *Kabbalah* and its teachings — no less than the *Halacha* — are an integral part of *Torah*. They are traced back to the historical roots of Sinai, part and parcel of *Moshe kibel Torah miSinai umesarah* ... (Moses received the Torah from Sinai and transmitted it...).

To be sure, in various works of the *Kabbalah*, one can find reports of mystical experiences, visions, the supernatural — all those things and more which we normally link to mysticism. They are there, but they are not the essence or even a major part of the *Kabbalah*. At best they are effects, possibilities or potential effects, that may accompany a mystic's life. The authentic mystic, however, will not seek to manipulate, and will shun interfering with the natural order instituted by the Creator.

The authentic mystic seeks knowledge, understanding. He wants to "Know the G-d of your father," to fulfill the precept of "You shall know this day and consider in your heart that the Eternal He is G-d in Heaven above and upon the earth below — there is nothing else." He seeks to realize and understand this axiom not only as an intellectual affirmation of truth but as a living reality within the limits of his capacity — profoundly sensing the literal omnipresence of G-d, with a penetrating understanding and knowledge as much as possible.

The Authenticity of Kabbalah

Kabbalah is theology in the fullest sense — including ontology, cosmogony and cosmology. It is not speculative philosophy based on human insight nor theories derived from human reasoning. It is a study, as it were, of Divinity and of the relationship between G-d and His Creation, based on the premises of revealed truth.

The *Kabbalah* takes man beyond the normative understanding of reason. It goes beyond the exoteric part of *Torah* and transcends normative existence. It uncovers many of the infinite layers of the secrets of life, of Creation, of the soul, of the heavenly spheres. It penetrates beyond the garments and the body of the *Torah*. It is the very core and soul of *Torah*, the ultimate revelation of Divinity — exposing the inner meaning, effects and purpose of *Torah* and *mitzvot*. The illumination emanating from the *Kabbalah* ignites the soul of man, setting it on fire in the awareness of a deeper and higher reality. Its study and insights are themselves mystical experiences. The *Kabbalah* is all this — but always and exclusively within the context of *Torah*. As a body cannot function without a soul, so the soul is ineffective without the body. The soul of the *Torah* (*nistar*, the esoteric part of the *Torah*) can never be separated from the body of the *Torah* (*nigleh*, or exoteric parts: *Halachah*, the commandments and practices prescribed by the *Torah*). *Kabbalah* reduced to spiritual or philosophical symbolism, stripped from the observance of the *mitzvot*, is worthless mumbo-jumbo, an empty shell.

That is the first and foremost difference between Jewish mysticism and all other kinds and forms. That is why Jewish mysticism can never fall into the category of a cult.

The great mystics and philosophers outside Judaism, in

the East and in the West, were honest and sincere sages. They did seek truth. They did not look for answers to justify or verify any of their preconceived notions. They were not indulging their egos. And many did discover and develop profound theories and insights which stir the imagination and move the human spirit. Some had glimpses of ultimate reality. Yet, in spite of all this, they worked in a chameleonic void. They could move only as far as finite and fallible man is able to reach on his own. Their insights or findings, therefore, are either humanly verifiable (that is, logically self-evident truth or tautologies) or else speculative truth which at best contains an element of possibility but never the assurance of certitude.

The *Kabbalah*, on the other hand, builds on the revealed truth of *Torah*. The validity of its speculative theories and subjective experiences must be, and is, tested and verified by that truth in order to be worthy of consideration, to be viable and acceptable. It has, and continually uses, objective criteria to make it consistent with, and as reliable as, *Halachah*.

Conclusion

At this point, though, we must realize that Jewish mysticism — the *Kabbalah and Chassidism* — is not just a legitimate and respectable part and dimension of authentic Judaism, of *Torah*.

The *Torah* is an organism, a complete whole in which every part is most intimately interrelated and interwoven with every other part; in which everything is interdependent upon everything else. The *Torah* is an organism analogous and parallel to, and in complete interaction with, the organism of the universe in general and the organism of man in particular. No part or particle, therefore, can be taken in isolation from the others.

Thus, even as it is incumbent upon each and every one of us to pursue the study and practice of the "body" of the *Torah* — *Halachah*; *mitzvot* — so it is obligatory and essential for each and every one of us to pursue the study and inspiration of the "soul" and fruits of the *Torah* and its interpretation.

To be sure, each of us is limited by his or her natural capacities. No one can absorb the totality of the *Torah* in its Divine infinity. But everyone can and must actualize his or her own potential, can and must reach out as far as his or her abilities can take them.

In fact, nowadays more than ever before, there is a most urgent need for the illumination and inspiration of the mystical dimension of the *Torah*. This very need is the great vision and contribution of the *Baal Shem Tov* and *Chassidism*. This very need is the purpose of this evening and the purpose of all the events of our Symposium on Jewish Mysticism.

These events were not meant to be another series of lectures for intellectual stimulation and academic knowledge. If they do not lead to practical consequences, if they will not inspire practical results and enhance spiritual and moral consciousness, then they may very well have been a waste of time.

The purpose of it all is to become linked with the Ultimate Essence, even if only in some small way. For essence is indivisible, and as the *Baal Shem Tov* taught: "When you grasp even a part of essence, you are holding all of it!"

* * *

*Rabbi Zusya of Annopol, one of the great masters of
Chassidism, said: "When my day comes and I will
stand before the Heavenly Throne of Judgment, I
shall be asked: 'Zusya! Why were you not as good and
great as the patriarchs — Abraham, Isaac and Jacob?'*

*"But I shall not be scared by that question. I will
answer quite simply: 'How can I be compared to
them? I am but a simple person without any special
qualities. The Patriarchs were holy men, like unto
angels, endowed with sublime souls. There is no
comparison whatsoever. The question is altogether
unfair!'*

*"The same answer will apply to any other compar-
ison with ancient or recent saints. I do not fear
questions like these. One thing, though, I am very
much afraid of and have no excuse for, namely, when
I shall be asked: 'Zusya, why were you not Zusya?'"*

We are not asked to ascend into the high heavens nor to
traverse the wide seas. We are not asked to become what we
are not. All we are asked to do is to be ourselves: to be true to
ourselves; to actualize our own true nature, our own abilities, our individual missions in life.

This is what it is all about, and the rest is but commentary. So now let us go forth and study — "to comprehend
and to discern, to perceive, to learn and to teach, to observe,
to practice and to fulfill all the teachings of G-d's *Torah*
with love."

Chabad Psychology and the Benoni of Tanya

Dr. Yitzchak Block

Although the *Tanya*, the magnum opus of Rabbi Schneur Zalman of Liadi, founder of Chabad-Lubavitch Chassidism, is the authoritative text of *Chabad Chassidism*, it still remains a closed book to many Jews today — even the intellectually minded with an interest in *Chassidism.* The reason for this is the book's unfamiliar, almost technical terminology. Nonetheless, the concepts themselves are most relevant to the modern Jew, searching as he is for "philosophical orientation." The purpose of the present article is to present one of the basic notions of the *Tanya* in a language closer to the understanding of the contemporary Jew. Unfortunately, limitations of space necessitate that the ideas and concepts introduced here be simplified. This article intends no more than to point out the general direction of *Chabad* thought on the topics discussed and does not attempt anything like a full exposition of them.

Chabad Psychology

When we call some aspects of *Chabad* thought "psychology," we do not mean to identify this with empirical psychology of either the behavioristic or clinical sort (though some leading ideas of *Chabad* bear resemblance to concepts behind modern psychoanalytic theory). It must be said, however, that *Chabad* psychology is not a science in the sense that modern psychoanalytic theory might be called a science. For in *Chabad* the discovery of forces behind conscious experience is not the result of empirical investigation; *Chabad* doctrines have their source in traditional *Talmudic* literature, *Midrash* and *Kabbalah*. The point at which *Chabad* and psychoanalytic theory converge is the notion that conscious experience, even at the level of higher thought-processes, is not the first link in the chain of mental events that compose our minds but is in the middle or towards the end. The origin of our thoughts and conscious feelings is the motivations, drives and forces that are unknown to ourselves. Our real personality is rooted in the unconscious, and what we call personality is a manifestation of something beneath the surface, as unknown to us as it is to a stranger. However, while psychoanalysis arrived at its notion of the unconscious through the clinical observations of Freud and others, *Chabad* posits the nature of the unconscious by appeal to traditional *Torah* literature and on this *a priori* basis attempts to explain the observable phenomena of inner experience and conflict within the Jew. In this enterprise, it has been remarkably successful; and one of the strongest appeals that *Chabad* has for the non-initiate is the *prima facie* plausibility of its psychological theory and the insight it brings to distinctively Jewish, inner experience. What we call *Chabad* "psychology" then is an explanation of the internal life of the Jew in his spiritual growth or decline.

As regards the psychology of the non-Jew, *Chabad*

maintains that it is distinct and is not susceptible to the same kind of analysis. The differences are not noticeable at the superficial level of "ordinary" experience but become more pronounced the deeper one delves into the personality. Our purpose here is not to argue this point but to note that the particular aspect of *Chabad* psychology discussed here is relevant only to the Jew. Other aspects of *Chabad* psychology not taken up in this article have a wider application.

The Benoni of Tanya

In the opening chapters of *Tanya* we find discussed the familiar tripartite division of *tzaddik* (righteous), *rasha* (wicked), and *benoni* (intermediate) and there is a concerted effort to define them, culminating in chapters 10-12. Though the *benoni* is the main object of exposition as we shall indicate, the fundamental division is between *tzaddik* on the one hand and the *benoni* and the *rasha* on the other. The *tzaddik* represents a character essentially different from the *benoni* or *rasha*, while the distinction between the *rasha* and the *benoni* is one of degree and not of kind. Nonetheless, it is around the *benoni* that the exposition develops. Aside from the fact that the sub-title reads "The Book of the Benonim," the central exhortation of the *Tanya* is to move one to seek the level of the *benoni* as indicated by the quotation with which the *Tanya* begins: "It has been taught (*Talmud, Niddah*, end chapter 3): an oath is administered to him [before birth, warning him] 'be righteous and not wicked; and even if the whole world tells you that you are righteous, regard yourself as if you are wicked.'" Though the *benoni* is not mentioned in this oath, its real significance, as explained in chapter 14, is directed to the category of the *benoni*. In addition it should be noted that the descriptions of the *tzaddik* in chapter 10 and the *rasha* in chapter 11 precede and act as groundwork for the explication of the *benoni* in chapter 12. By analyzing the *benoni* then, we will be gaining insight into the fundamental notion of the *Tanya*. Intimately connected with this, however, is the proper understanding of the distinction between the personalities of the *tzaddik* and the *benoni*, and therefore discussion of these two points must proceed in conjunction with one another.

The normal Jew is a split personality drawn in different and antagonistic directions. The resolution of the split into a "whole" personality occurs only in extreme cases, i.e., in the *tzaddik* or else in one entirely evil. But conflict is the inherited lot of the normal Jew, and the source of this conflict is the inborn powers of good and evil. The terms "good" and "evil" are used in a wide variety of contexts, mainly non-Jewish, and will certainly be misconstrued unless further explicated. Here they have a simple and straightforward meaning: good is that which draws a man closer to G-d and evil is that which inclines him away from G-d. The term for evil in *Kabbalah* is *sitra achra* — the other side, i.e., that side of the world that is not essentially connected with holiness and G-d. The world, then, is dichotomized into the G-dly and the un-G-dly. There exists a middle ground with a mixture of the two and is called, in *kabbalistic* terms, *kelipat nogah*. However, *kelipat nogah*, — "impurity with a ray of goodness" — is unstable and ultimately resolves into its irreducible elements of good and evil.

Though cosmological forces permeate the entire universe, the forces of good and evil have a particularized relationship as they manifest themselves in the life of a Jew. The dictum that man is a miniature world in himself[1] is interpreted to mean that just as there is a cosmological struggle between good and evil in the world at large, so too in the Jew is there a similar struggle. The forces in this conflict are termed in *Chabad* literature *nefesh elokit* (the G-dly soul) and *nefesh habehamit* (the animal soul)[2]. They battle for control over the individual as two armies for a military objective. In other words, a Jew does not have merely one soul but two, both fully armed with equivalent powers and functions; the G-dly soul seeks that man desire only the holy and the good; and the animal soul, that man be drawn by his appetites to evil.

This concept of personality leads *Chabad* to judge certain acts leniently. One who steals and gives the money to charity is not false or hypocritical but in the throes of a struggle. At one time one force prevails; at another time, the other. Similarly, on a more refined level, the Jew who prays but has his mind on his business is not properly termed dishonest but one whose energies are dispersed in different directions. One power leads him to pray, while another draws his mind away from G-d at that very moment.

At this point the question arises, what is the prize of this struggle? If each soul has its own powers, what does the victor gain other than the corpse of the vanquished? This question is answered in various ways in *Chabad* literature. Sometimes our power to choose is described as neutral and can be drawn to both good and evil. However, there is a more predominant position upon which we shall focus.

According to *Chabad* the most external aspects of personality are thought, speech and action. These functions are not essential aspects of the soul but are different media whereby the more internal powers of the soul are revealed. They are the "garments" of the soul — *levushei hanefesh* — ways that the soul shows itself to the world. Though conscious thought is closer to the soul and a more genuine expression of its nature than either speech or action, it is nonetheless merely an external expression of deeper aspects. More central are powers that in Chabad are termed Intellect (*sechel*) and Feeling (*midot*). Actually, these powers are also not the *essence* of the soul, which is unknowable; however, in relationship to the "garments," they can be considered as the essence for they are the body that the more external functions clothe. Thought, speech and deeds are ways that Intellect and Feeling manifest themselves. One can express one's mind by thinking, speaking or acting; and Feeling can show itself in these three ways as well. Intellect and Feeling themselves, however, are distinct from thought, speech or action.

These three powers can be put on or taken off at will as one decides which suit to wear. To continue the analogy, just as two people can wear the same suit (at different moments), so the two souls can dress themselves at different times in these three powers, and this is the prize of the contest between the two souls. When good triumphs, one's thoughts, speech and action are connected with G-d; and when evil wins, these powers are disassociated from G-d and become agents of evil. There is no stable middle ground or no-man's land. Man has control over how he shall utilize his thought, speech and power of action; however, he has little to say in the formation and character of his Intellect and Feeling. A person can have some effect on his Intellect and Feeling by great effort and discipline over a protracted period of time. A man can transform himself, in a sense, as we shall see in the case of the *tzaddik*. For the most part, however, they are fixed and set by heredity or early environment.

Now we can better understand the distinction between the *tzaddik* and the *benoni* or the *rasha*. The *benoni* and the *rasha* struggle at the level of thought, speech or action, while the *tzaddik* has destroyed the initial conflict by having transformed himself at the level of Intellect and Feeling. He has eradicated the aspect of Intellect and Feeling connected with the animal soul and only the Intellect and Feeling of the G-dly soul operate. The notions of Intellect and Feeling cannot be described here in detail and must, unfortunately, remain vague. Suffice it to say that Intellect and Feeling come to the fore in conscious experience, but they have their immediate roots in the unconscious. Intellect, in particular, remains for the most part an aspect of our unconscious. This is one of the reasons the *benoni* cannot by pure self-discipline root out the evil counterparts of these powers. In the *tzaddik*, this is accomplished primarily by a special act of favor from G-d.

However, what is relevant to the Jew is his thought, speech and action — the external garments that he controls and through which all *mitzvot* are carried out. The *benoni* is one who constantly struggles with the evil within himself, and while never completely vanquishing it, he never allows it to utilize his external powers as instruments. The *benoni* is the epitome of mastery and self-discipline.

If the concern of the *benoni* is to bind his thought, speech and action to G-d, he must know with some precision just what kind of mental activity, words and deeds will accomplish this. *Chabad* and traditional *chassidic* thought are quite specific at this point and it is here that modern interpreters such as Buber and Heschel diverge from genuine *chassidic* teaching. These writers may describe the broad lines of spiritual struggle underscored by *chassidism* and its general orientation, but they deny, implicitly or explicitly, the means whereby *chassidism* insists its goals are attained. It is a fundamental cornerstone of *chassidism* and traditional Jewish thought that the *Torah* represents the Wisdom of G-d and that obedience to the commandments constitutes fulfillment of His Will. Thus, thought and speech are connected with G-d in the study and oral discussion of *Torah*, and one's deeds are linked with G-d by the scrupulous performance of the *mitzvot*. Modern writers on *chassidism* are inclined to consider this a mere carry-over from the legal or rabbinic tradition against which *chassidism* was supposed to have been a "rebellion." This is false. The belief that *Torah* and *mitzvot* represent G-d's Wisdom and Will in a literal sense is an integral part of *chassidic* thought with its source in *Kabbalah* and the writings of Rabbi Isaac Luria.

The G-dly soul will impel a man to the study of *Torah* and the practice of the *mitzvot*, while the animal soul will draw him after physical pleasure, for such is the animal instinct. Evil in man is the drive to satisfy physical desire and it is this that severs the connection between man and G-d and leads him to transgress. "No man sins without benefit to himself" (*Talmud, Baba Metzia 5b*), and "No man sins unless there enters into him the spirit of folly" (*Talmud, Sotah 3a*). These two *Talmudic* sayings are complementary, for it is folly to suppose that material gain or physical pleasure is worth the price of transgression.

This disdain for physical pleasure should not be interpreted as an appeal to asceticism. To utilize and derive benefit from the physical world is not evil. On the contrary, the *mitzvot* can be performed only with the aid of material things. What is evil is the desire for the *pleasure* that material things can give. Satisfaction of needs and desire for material possessions in order to serve G-d consecrates the material world and hallows it. This, indeed, is the reason why the *mitzvot* require utilization of the material world.

This doctrine of the rejection of physical pleasure does not sit well with contemporary Jewish thinking and some attempt to brand it as non-Jewish. How fundamental this doctrine is and what is involved in its denial can be seen from an analysis of the emotions of love and hate as *Chabad* conceives them.

The ultimate goal of the spiritual life is love of G-d. Since love and hatred are complementary in the sense that one hates that which separates him from the object of his love, love for G-d is accompanied by hatred for that which separates one from Him. According to *Chabad*, love for G-d is a characteristic of the Feeling aspect of the G-dly soul, while love for physical pleasure is a quality of the Feeling aspect of the animal soul. These being antagonistic in their very nature, the love for physical pleasure in a sense stifles the love for G-d. This is the proper interpretation of the passage in the *Zohar*: "When the body becomes strong the soul becomes weak, and when the soul becomes strong the body becomes weak" (*Zohar, Part I, 140b and 180b*). This does not mean that one must cause the body physical harm or weaken it by abstinence, for this is considered a grievous sin in *chassidic* thought as expressed in the words of the Maggid of Mezeritch: "When one makes a tiny hole in the body, one makes a big hole in the soul." Bodily health is necessary for spiritual health and what is meant in the *Zohar* is that when one is drawn after the desires of the body, the desires of the spirit or the G-dly soul are weakened accordingly, and a strengthening of the spirit entails a weakening of the attractive power of physical pleasure.

If this doctrine is valid, one who loves G-d must have an equivalent hatred for physical pleasure. This is certainly unnatural, but it is the proper description of the *tzaddik* according to the *Tanya* (*chapter 10*). He has not only removed himself from evil by refraining from evil thoughts, words or deeds, but he has also removed evil from himself by having transformed the Intellect and Feeling of the animal soul and converted them to good. The *tzaddik* thus stands above conflict and strife. His abiding love for G-d is matched by an equally profound hatred for physical pleasure. This is a personality separate and distinct from the *benoni* and *rasha* who have all the desires and attractions of ordinary mortals. Since the *benoni* has not yet fused the Intellect and Feeling of the animal soul to become one with the G-dly soul, he is drawn by the instinctive attraction of bodily pleasure with which he constantly contends. Accordingly, his love for G-d cannot be genuine or permanent but only fleeting and temporary. The *tzaddik's* personality, on the other hand, no longer contains a "split." It is conflict-free and whole by virtue of the transformation of the animal soul. The *tzaddik* is unique and cannot properly be compared with a "typical" human personality.

But if the *tzaddik* is the ultimate goal of life as *chassidism* conceives it, why is the *Tanya* addressed primarily to the *benoni*? The answer reveals a unique characteristic of *Chabad*. Most *chassidic* legends center around the person of the *tzaddik*, and many of these stories should be more significant in light of the little we have said here. However, *Chabad* has always stressed that every Jew without exception must improve his own inner, spiritual life each day. Not everyone has equal abilities in this regard, but whatever the capacities an individual possesses must be utilized today in lifting one's spirit a little higher than it was yesterday. One will probably not become a *tzaddik*: "For G-d has seen the righteous and they are few" (*Talmud, Yoma 38b*), and one may not even attain the level of the *benoni* — no mean accomplishment. However, this is not the immediate concern. For the point is to raise oneself a little higher in the realm of thought, speech and action. This is in the hands of every Jew, and the highest plane that one can reach by one's own effort in this manner is the *benoni*. If G-d sees fit, He then bestows upon him the blessing of the *tzaddik*, but this is G-d's business, so to speak. One must be practical, though, and try to gain what can be accomplished here and now. It is the primary concern of the *Tanya* to serve as a guide to each Jew in this enterprise. It is a handbook in spiritual improvement that has something to say to everyone and points to a goal within reach.

---

1. *Midrash Tanchuma, Pekudei* 3.
2. See *Tanya* Chapter 9.

The Mystical Meaning of Shabbat

Rabbi Adin Steinsaltz

Holiness, manifested in time, comes as consecrated days in the week, the month and the year. The concept of time according to the Jewish way of thinking is not that of a linear flow that passes; it is a process in which past, present and future are bound to each other, not only by cause and effect but also as a harmonization of two movements — of progress forward, and a counter-motion backwards, encircling and returning. It is more like a spiral, or a helix, rising up from Creation. There is always a certain return to the past, and the past is never a state that has gone and is no more. It is rather always returning and beginning again at a particular significant point, the significance of which changes constantly according to changing circumstances. There is thus a constant reversing to basic patterns of the past, although it is never possible to have a precise counterpart of any moment of time.

The scope of this return to the past is diverse, the movement ranging through a number of circles intersecting, and interlocking with one another. The primary circuit is that of day and night. Thereafter are the week, the month and the year, the half-century cycles of the jubilee and the great cycles of a thousand years and of seven thousand years.

The round of the week is connected to the seven days of Creation, being a sort of methodological recapitulation of Genesis. Each day of the week is not only an occasion to mark the particular work of creation of that day, it is also a framework for manifesting the special quality of existence corresponding to one of the *sefirot*. For, as it would appear, the seven days and the particular thing created in each of the days of Genesis are emanations of the higher *sefirot* into time. Thus there are days of the week that belong to certain kinds of action or states of mind; other days are fit for, and respond to, other modes of being. Tuesday, for example, being the manifestation of the *sefirah* of *Tiferet* (Beauty or Harmony) is considered a day prone to success and good fortune. While Monday, the day of the *sefirah* of *Gevurah* (Strength or Justice) and Wednesday are considered to have a deleterious severity about them.

Also the hours and portions of the day have their rhythmic patterns according to the subtle influences of the *sefirot* as reflected by the slanting rays of the sun. The morning comprises the well-favored hours, the afternoon is largely under the influence of the *sefirah* of *Gevurah* becoming ever more stern and hard with the oncoming of evening; while the time from midnight to dawn is the time for manifestation of the finer and gentler qualites of *Tiferet*.

The Shabbat is not just another day of the week, or even a special day; it sums up the week and gives meaning to it. The weekdays are marked by the acts of Creation, ever-repeated by the descent of the divine plenty into the world. And parallel to it, during the week it is man's function, in the order of things, to fix and to set the world right wherever it tends to go wrong. This includes correcting the world in the physical sense by work and action on the external frame, and in the spiritual sense perfecting the world by performing *mitzvot.* For in the realm of the human soul, man's work on himself, his constant correcting of faults and the mending and activation of his inner being, constitute an incessant creative effort.

The Shabbat is essentially the day of rest, of cessation from all labor and creative effort. And this holds true for the spiritual effort of working on oneself as well as for the physical effort of working on the world. The week is characterized by being busy or active, while the Shabbat is grounded on stillness, on the nullification of oneself in the downpour of holiness. And this self-repudiation is expressed by a renunciation of all work: whether it be in the physical sense, by being busy in the world; or in the spiritual sense, by the efforts to correct one's soul. In fact, the very power to receive the spiritual essence of the Shabbat comes from one's readiness and ability to surrender, to give up one's human and worldly state for the sake of the supreme holiness, through which all the worlds are raised to a higher level.

The round of weekdays and Shabbats is without end. On one hand, the weekdays prepare for the Shabbat, providing additional plenty to the world and correcting the world, making it possible to bring things to a conclusion and to raise them to a suitably higher level. On the other hand, the Shabbat is the source of plenty for all the days of the week that follow it. The surrender of oneself on the Shabbat is not a matter of non-activity but an opening of oneself to the influence of the higher worlds and thereby receiving the strength for all the days of the week that follow.

This sanctity of a day, a certain unit of time, is — like the sanctity of a place — intrinsic to it. It cannot be transferred to another day. Nevertheless, the experiencing of this holiness, objective as it is, depends on one's spiritual readiness and openness. The more intensive and sincere the preparations during the week in the secular course of a person's life, the more holy is the Shabbat. The higher the spiritual level of a person in general, the more keenly is the sense of the general uplift — a raising of all the worlds — felt on this day. Thus, although the round of the weekdays and the Shabbat is endlessly repeated, it is never the same. There are subtle variations in the flow of plenty, just as men themselves differ. And still, every single week is an archetype, a recapitulation of the primordial pattern of Genesis.

The eve of the Shabbat has its own particular aspect of the Seventh Day. Every hour of the preceding afternoon marks another level of the transition from the six working days of the week to the Shabbat day of rest. The Shabbat Eve itself is the final stage of the transition to the two aspects of the Holy Day as the conclusion of the week and as the higher level of existence, beyond the six days of action, beyond time.

This higher level of the Shabbat is bound up with the divine manifestation in the *sefirah* of *Malchut* (Kingdom) which represents the *Shechinah*, and also the totality, the receptacle that absorbs all that occurs, as well as being the last *sefirah*, the Crown. Therefore the quality of Shabbat Eve, which is the summing up of work and events in time, can also be a preparation for the manifestation of the Shabbat itself, as the crown and beginning of time. The *sefirah* of *Malchut*, or the *Shechinah*, represents the Divine power as manifested in reality in greatly varied ways and means. She has seventy names, each expressing another aspect, another face of this all inclusive *sefirah*. For *Malchut* is the seventh of the lower *sefirot* and being the last, also includes in herself the entire ten. In other words, she expresses all of the *sefirot*, each in seven different forms, so that seventy is the key number to the unfolding of the ritual of the evening devoted as it is to *Malchut*, and to the *Shechinah* which *Malchut* represents.

To be sure there is something equal in all the manifestations of the *Shechinah*, all having a certain aspect of the feminine, so that the symbols and the contents of the evening of Shabbat are always female-oriented with emphasis on the woman, in universal terms as in terms of the Jewish family.

On entering a home on the evening of the Shabbat, that which stands out, more than at any other time, is how the dwelling place of a man may be made into a sanctuary. The table on which the white loaves of Shabbat bread and the burning candles are set recall the Holy Temple with its showbreads and its menorah. The table itself is, as always, a reminder of the altar in the Temple, for eating could and should become an act of sacrifice. In other words, the relationship between man and the food he consumes and the intention behind the eating of the food constitutes the same connection between the material and the spiritual in all the worlds, which exists also in every sacrifice on an altar. This is more so on the Shabbat when the Shabbat feast is itself a sacramental act, a sort of communion, a performing of the *mitzvah* of the union of the soul, the body, the food and the essence of holiness. Therefore the table always has on it, at mealtimes, a container of salt, just as there had to be salt on the altar as a sign of the covenant of salt. The candles, lit by the woman of the house, emphasize the light of the Shabbat, the sanctification of the day and the special task of the woman in the Shabbat as representative of *Shechinah*, of *Malchut*. There are two loaves of special white bread, *challah*, (some houses have twelve *challot*) covered with a cloth, recalling the bread from heaven, the Manna, which came down in double portions on *erev* Shabbat, and the layer of dew which was to be found under it and over it, so that there is the cloth covering the bread on all sides.

As part of the preparations for the *Kiddush* (sanctification) ceremony, the members of the household sing or recite the song of praise for the "woman of valor" (*Proverbs 31:10-31*). The song with its admiring phrases for the woman, the mother, the housekeeper, has on this Shabbat evening a double connotation, both as praise for the lady of the house and as glorification of the *Shechinah*, of *Malchut*, who is in a sense the mother, housekeeper of the real world. Following this, we recite psalm 23 expressing calm trust in G-d. One is then ready for the *Kiddush* ceremony itself.

In terms of the *halachah*, the *Kiddush* is the carrying out of the fourth of the Ten Commandments: "Remember the Shabbat Day to keep it holy." So that at the very beginning of the Shabbat there has to be some act of separation, of sanctification, emphasizing the difference between the rest of the week and the holy day and enabling the soul to move into a state of inner tranquility and spiritual receptiveness. To be sure, the words of the sanctification are also said at the time of evening prayer and on other occasions. But in Judaism there is a general principle that abstract events or processes, and all that pertains to them, are to as great an extent as possible bound up with specific contents and very definite actions. So, the *Kiddush* sanctification is connected with the drinking of wine, which in turn becomes part of a ceremony and, in turn, is associated with the Shabbat wine sacrifices of the Holy Temple.

The *Kiddush* cup symbolizes the vessel through which, and into which, the blessing comes. The numerical value of the letters of the word for drinking cup (*kos*) equals the numerical value for the letters of the name of G-d which expresses the Divine revelation in the world, in nature, in law. And into the cup is poured the bounty, the wine that represents the power of the blessing of the word "wine." Also the numerical equivalent, that is, the sum of its letter-numbers, is seventy, which is the number of Shabbat evening, as mentioned. Wine then evokes the bounty, the great plentitude and power. Red wine especially expresses a certain aspect of the *sefirah* of *Gevurah* (power) when it stands by itself. But it also has an aspect of justice, so that after one has poured most of the wine into the cup, a little water (symbol of grace and love) is added to create the right mixture, or harmony, between *Chesed* and *Gevurah*. The cup, which is now the vessel of sanctification, filled with the divine plenty is then placed on the palm of the right hand in such a way that it is supported by the upturned fingers, resembling a sort of rose of five petals. For one of the symbols of *Malchut* is the rose. And the cup of wine, expressing the *Shechinah*, stands in the center of the palm and is held by the petal fingers of the rose. The time has come for the recitation of the *Kiddush* prayer.

The *Kiddush* is composed of two parts. It begins with that part of the *Torah* (*Genesis 2:1-3*) in which the Shabbat is first mentioned. The second half consists of a prayer composed by the Sages especially for the *Kiddush* and in which the various meanings of the Shabbat are poetically and precisely stated. Between the two parts there is the blessing on the wine, fruit of the grape. In each of these two parts there are exactly thirty-five words, together making seventy, the numerical value of Shabbat evening. Before the first words from the *Torah*, two words are added. These are the last words of the preceding verse: "*Yom Hashishi*" (the sixth day) because they fit in with the statement: "Thus the heavens and the earth were finished..." and also because the first letters of these two Hebrew words form the abbreviation of the Holy name. In this first section the Shabbat is treated from the viewpoint of G-d, as the day of the summation and cessation of creation. It is G-d's day of rest and therefore deserves to be a separate section.

The second section, selected and determined by the Sages, expresses the other side of the Shabbat, the imitation of G-d by Israel. Before the blessing on the wine, there are the two words in Aramaic: "*Savrei Maranan*" telling those present to prepare for the blessing. The following words of the *Kiddush* express the primary elements of the Shabbat and the special relationship between the Shabbat and the nation. By commencing with the words: "Blessed art Thou... by whose commandments we are sanctified," one acknowledges that the *mitzvah* is a way of reaching a level of holiness, a way to G-d. Then the emphasis is on G-d's choice of Israel from among all the other nations to assume the special task of carrying on the act of creation, and its aftermath of rest and holiness. Mention is made of the Exodus from Egypt, as in the version of the Ten Commandments in *Deuteronomy 5:15* where the Shabbat is proclaimed also as a day of rest from work. Recollecting the time of slavery in Egypt likens the Shabbat to the Divine act of release and salvation which brings freedom. Shabbat is therefore the day for freedom in the week and a memorial to the release and exodus from Egypt. It exemplifies the concept of the final salvation, which is the Shabbat of the world.

Arising from this emphasis on Divine choice and love, of the need to understand man's obligation to G-d to continue to create and to be able to rise above and beyond creation to the Shabbat rest, the *Kiddush* concludes with the relationship of the Jewish people to the institution of the Shabbat, closing the circle of the relationship between G-d and man. After the recital of the *Kiddush*, the one who performs the ceremony drinks from the cup, thereby participating in that communion between the physical and the spiritual which is the essence of all ritual. And from the same cup drink all those gathered at the table, so that each and everyone may also participate in the same meaningful act of introducing the Shabbat, represented by the flowering of the rose which is the cup of redemption of the individual and of the nation and of the world as a whole.

Practical Implications of Infinity

Rabbi Dr. Jonathan Sacks

What is mysticism? The word conjures up connotations of lofty abstraction, other-worldly meditation, abstruse speculations into the meaning of existence, a world apart from, perhaps even opposed to, the mundane and prosaic questions that make up the texture of daily life.

If that is so, what does mysticism have to do with Judaism? It is, after all, the defining feature of Judaism, which some praise, others criticize, that its concern is with the small details of conduct. Though it is other things as well, Judaism is supremely the *Halachah*, the open-ended rules for decision-making in practical contexts. Perhaps the subtitle that the first Lubavitcher Rebbe gave to his classic work *Tanya — Sefer shel Benonim*, the Book for the Average Man — is the aptest of descriptions of Judaism as a whole. The *Torah* is a book for the average man in average situations. And surely, almost by definition, a mystic is not an average man; his vision is anything but the norm.

In many places the *Torah* itself, and certainly the rabbis in their comments upon it, insists upon this fact, that the law it contains is not lofty, remote or esoteric:

> *For this commandment which I command you this*

> *day, is not hidden from you, nor is it far away. It is*
> *not in Heaven, that you should say: Who shall go up*
> *for us to heaven, and bring it to us, that we may hear*
> *it and do it? . . . But the thing is very near to you, in*
> *your mouth and in your heart, that you may do it.*
> [Deuteronomy 30:11-14]

The Sages were fond of saying: "The *Torah* was not given to ministering angels" (*Talmud, Berachot 25b*). The *Talmud* describes a dialogue between Moses and the angels when he ascended to Heaven to receive the *Torah*. The angels protested: how could the most precious of Divine treasures be handed over to man? Moses replied with a long string of rhetorical questions:

> *Did you go down to Egypt? Were you enslaved to*
> *Pharaoh? Why then should the* Torah *be yours? . . .*
> *Do you perform work that you need the* Shabbat *as a*
> *day of rest? Do you have business dealings that you*
> *need a law against falsehood? Is there jealousy*
> *amongst you that you need rules against murder and*
> *theft?* [Talmud, Shabbat 88b-89a]

Moses descends, victorious. The *Torah* is not for beings who are perfect. It is not for those who live above the problems of ordinary human life.

So our question returns: What has mysticism to do with Judaism? It could be said, and convincingly, that Judaism needs a mystical dimension. Do we not dress in white and refrain from eating and drinking on *Yom Kippur* in imitation of the ministering angels? There are times, especially in prayer, when we must commune with the Infinite. It would be a pale shadow of a religious existence if there were no place for meditating on "He who spoke and the world came into being" and no time for thinking of "He who teaches *Torah* to His people, Israel.'' In fulfilling the *mitzvot* we would be like someone who keeps the command of the king while forgetting that there is a king.

But our concern here is with a more significant issue than the dimension of depth that mysticism is.

The *Talmud*, which always relates intellectual issues to real choices, has a standard question when it is faced with a difference of opinion between two views. It asks: what is the *practical* difference? And this is our question. Does a mystical vision make a practical difference to the way we are bound to act in accordance with the *Halachah*? What are the practical implications of infinity?

Custom, beauty and law

It is one of the strange facts of the history of the Jewish mind that the great mystics have also been the great *halachists*. Their concern with infinity took them into some very finite areas indeed. To mention only the most familiar names: Joseph Caro, author of the *Shulchan Aruch*, was a member of the great mystical circle in Tzefat. R. Schneur Zalman of Liadi, the first Rebbe of Lubavitch, is as well-known for his code of law, the *Shulchan Aruch HaRav*, as for his mystical writings. Perhaps the greatest of all the early rabbinic teachers, R. Akiva, whose methods shaped the whole development of the *Halachah*, was a profound mystic whose views sometimes perplexed, sometimes scandalized his contemporaries.

This mysticism/*Halachah* connection (for which a whole string of names can be adduced) is all the more striking compared with the other approach to resolving the fundamental questions of religion: philosophy. Of the great

Jewish philosophers who were distinguished as *halachists*, only the name of Moses Maimonides stands out, with perhaps the lesser figure of Rav Saadia Gaon.

The reason lies deep. But for a single-sentence summary it would perhaps be fair to say that while the philosopher attaches great significance to great truths, the mystic attaches it to small ones as well. Since every fragment of the infinite is also infinite, perhaps also it could be said that while the philosopher thinks his way towards G-d, the mystic experiences and lives his way. For the mystic every detail of the *mitzvah* is important. And hence his concern with detail — the essence of the *Halachah*.

But did all this make a practical difference?

In some ways its impact was obvious. In the area of *minhag*, a great many Jewish customs are based upon considerations that are *kabbalistic*: the way we hold the *kiddush* cup or the double loaves of bread on *Shabbat*, for example; or the retention of *mayim acharonim* (the hand-washing at the conclusion of a meal) after the original reason ceased to apply. Perhaps the most dramatic incursion of a *kabbalistic* practice into the normal routines of Judaism is the *kabbalat Shabbat* service on Friday evenings before *maariv*. The *Lecha Dodi* song and the turning at the end to meet the *Shabbat* bride coming from the direction of the setting sun — all originate from the sixteenth-century mystics in Tzefat.

Again, the mystics attached great significance to what is known as *hiddur mitzvah* (performing a precept in the most beautiful manner possible). This is an ancient concept:

> *This is my G-d and I will beautify Him* [Exodus 15:2] *— make yourselves beautiful before Him in the fulfillment of the commands. Make a beautiful* succah, *a beautiful* lulav, *a beautiful* shofar, *beautiful* tzitzit

and a beautiful Sefer Torah, *write it with fine ink, a fine pen, a skilled scribe, and wrap it around with beautiful silks.* [Talmud, Shabbat 133b]

Nonetheless it received a prominence amongst the mystics, certainly amongst *chassidim*, that it had not had hitherto.

But both custom and beautification, intensity and adornment, are themselves dimensions of depth within the basic framework of the *Halachah*. Given then that the mystics had a profound motivation to be interested in the details of Jewish law, and that they added to it refinements which went beyond the essential requirements, do we have instances where the mystical vision affected the *Halachah* itself, in the sense that, in response to specific practical issues, the answers which emerged did so because of a certain fundamental orientation towards the infinite dimension in existence?

R. Shimon bar Yochai and R. Judah bar Ilai

The figure whom Jewish tradition invests with the honor of being the grandfather of mysticism — not the first but the most influential — is R. Shimon bar Yochai. He was one of the greatest of the rabbis of the late *Mishnaic* period, and he is a dominating presence in the early rabbinic literature, in both *Halachah* and *aggadah*. Mysticism as such does not figure largely in the statements attributed to him in the *Talmud*: that belongs to the more esoteric literature of the *Zohar*. Nonetheless, a graphic picture of his personality emerges. He was a man of extremes, always uncompromising, always radical, a man for whom the study of the *Torah* transcended all else, and a man who cared nothing for the cliches of conventional wisdom.

The *Talmud* relates that, because of his opposition to the Roman government then in power in Israel, R. Shimon was forced to escape for his life and to take refuge in a cave, where he and his son lived for twelve years, oblivious to the hardship, and only concerned not to waste a moment of time that could be spent in studying *Torah*:

> *So they went and hid in a cave. A miracle occurred and a carob-tree and a well of water were created for them. They would take off their garments and sit up to their necks in sand. The whole day they studied. When it was time for prayer, they robed, covered themselves, prayed and then took off their garments again so that they should not wear out.* [Talmud, Shabbat 33b]

What is of interest to us here is: what occurred that R. Shimon had to escape from the Romans? The account given by the *Talmud* is intriguing:

> *R. Judah [bar Ilai], R. Yose and R. Shimon were sitting, and Judah ben Gerim was sitting near them. R. Judah began the discussion by saying: How fine are the works of this people [the Romans]. They have made streets, they have built bridges, they have constructed baths. R. Yose was silent. R. Shimon bar Yochai answered and said: All that they have made, they have done so for themselves. They built marketplaces to put harlots there; they made baths to rejuvenate themselves; they made bridges to levy tolls.* [ibid.]

Judah ben Gerim, who had overheard the conversation, reported it to the authorities. R. Judah, who had praised the Romans, was given official honor. R. Yose, who was silent, was sent into exile. R. Shimon, who had so castigated the achievements of the Romans, was sentenced to death.

It is fascinating, apart from the historical significance of the account, to overhear the two great rabbis, R. Judah and R. Shimon, who so often disagreed on matters of *Halachah*, this time debating a question of political and moral values. In the broadest sense, the opinions they expressed were consistent with all we know about these two personalities. But what, specifically, was the argument between them on this occasion? R. Judah was a politically sensitive individual, and there can be no doubt that he was fully aware of R. Shimon's truth, that behind the remarkable technological achievements of the Romans — feats of construction that are no less awe-inspiring today, in retrospect — lay moral bankruptcy. And R. Shimon, in turn, knew that what R. Judah said was true. What then divided them?

There are many possible ways of putting it. Amongst them, we will pursue just one line of thought. Namely, that R. Judah looked at the *facts*, and R. Shimon looked at the *intentions* that lay behind them. For R. Judah, a fact, an achievement, could be impressive in its own right. For R. Shimon the question was always, "To what end was this intended?" If it is a corrupt or self-centered one, then I refuse to be impressed. Because no evaluation of human creations can be made without a consideration of the purpose for which they were meant.

It is an argument which in other forms can be heard often today. There are those who argue, for example, that something can be considered a great work of art, even if it is morally objectionable, because it should be considered in itself and without reference to any wider context. And there are others who say, to the contrary, that the moral context must be considered before we can pronounce any judgment at all.

But does the argument between R. Judah and R. Shimon have anything to do with mysticism? In a superficial sense we could say that R. Judah looked at the concrete, physical facts, while R. Shimon looked instead at the realm of thought and intention. To this extent R. Shimon is interested in the intangible, while R. Judah focuses on the reality that is grasped by the physical senses.

But we must go deeper. What in general is the mystical vision? It is that reality lies deeper than the appearances presented to our senses. To express it in a way that is at least roughly true of the Jewish mystical tradition: the physical world conceals more than it reveals. Beneath all appearances lies the reality of the Infinite, the *Ein Sof*, that can neither be perceived nor described. *Chabad* philosophy, in particular, stresses the analogy between the way the world came into being and the way — in human psychology — in which an action develops out of thought and emotion. There is a sequence by which the glimmer of a thought is developed into a fully-fledged idea, is invested with emotion, and eventually turns into decision and action. Only the final stage of the process — the behavior — is seen by others. But its essential meaning lies way back, in the first flash of thought which set the process in motion. So, too, on a cosmic scale. The world, as we see it, is only the last stage of the process (*hishtalshelut*), and is like, in this respect, a human action (*olam ha'asiyah*). But if we were to travel backwards and inwards we would reach further towards the originating reality (*asiyah*, *yetzirah*, *beriah*, *atzilut*); perhaps back even beyond the first thought, to the personality that conceived it, and which is of course infinitely wider than any specific intention into which it is directed (*Ein Sof*).

If this analogy is to be taken in any way seriously, then a mystical vision that looks beyond the surface reality of the world must look beyond the surface reality of human behavior as well. It is not enough to look at the final outcome. The real meaning lies in the intention.

And so it happens that a deeply esoteric view of the nature of G-d and the universe may carry with it quite simple implications for the way we interpret human behavior. While R. Judah is content to look upon the glittering surface of Roman achievements, R. Shimon's restlessly searching mind takes him beyond, to the less than impressive intentions and qualities of the soul which set the civilization on its course. The mystic became a political radical.

Action and Intention

But politics is a large and abstract subject, even if at times the expression of an opinion can endanger one's life. Is the difference between R. Judah and R. Shimon one that has more practical consequences still?

It is. We find these two rabbis arguing about what, on the face of it, is a quite unrelated and seemingly trivial issue. As it happens, the passage in question has quite wide implications for the laws of *Shabbat* in general. But in its original formulation it reads as follows:

> R. Judah says: No articles may be dragged along the ground except a wagon, because it only presses the earth down... R. Shimon says: A man may drag along a bed, stool or bench across the ground, provided he had no intention of making a furrow. [Mishnah and Talmud, Betzah 23b; Tosefta, Betzah chapter 2; Talmud, Shabbat 29b and elsewhere]

This is the specific case. The general rule over which they disagree is:

> R. *Judah maintains that an unintentional act is forbidden; but R. Shimon holds that an unintentional act is permitted.* [Talmud, Betzah ibid.]

The question is this: someone does something on *Shabbat* which is, in itself, permitted — like dragging a chair along the earth. All he intends to do is to move the chair. But while he is doing so he may be making a furrow in the ground. And making a furrow is forbidden on *Shabbat*, either as a subsidiary case of building or of ploughing, two of the categories of forbidden labor.

In fact this kind of case is quite common nowadays. For example: we open a refrigerator on *Shabbat* to take out some food. It may happen that the cooling mechanism is not operative at the moment when we open the door, but the sudden in-rush of warm air causes it to start up. We did not intend to start the motor. All we intended to do was to take out the food. Nonetheless, the consequence was, in fact, that the motor started. And to start a motor is certainly to transgress the *Shabbat*.

What is the law in such cases? Is the act permitted because in itself it is innocent? Or is it forbidden because it may have consequences that are forbidden? R. Judah and R. Shimon disagree. But by now it should be apparent that their disagreement is — strangely enough — of exactly the same form as their difference of opinion on the Romans. For R. Judah looks at the facts. And R. Shimon looks at the intentions. At the end of the day, argues R. Judah, the person who dragged the chair made a furrow, and that is forbidden. But, counters R. Shimon, he did not intend to make the furrow, and what counts is his intention. The law, on this question, follows R. Shimon.

And so we have traced, in a direct line, an orientation of thought that has moved from mysticism to politics to the laws of *Shabbat*. And it has made a difference. R. Shimon did not merely, because of his mysticism, think of *Shabbat* in terms of an extra dimension of depth: that it was not just a day of rest, but a day in which the spiritual rifts in Creation were healed. The *Shechinah* came temporarily out of its exile, and peace reigned in the Heavenly orders. He also gave practical rulings that followed from his premises; they differed from those of R. Judah and they were taken up as law.

Expounding the reasons of the Torah

Let us move on to quite another kind of question. A major facet of the *halachic* process is attempting to determine the precise meaning of the commands stated in the *Torah*. And this is not always a simple procedure. For what principles are we to use in interpreting the Bible?

On this question, too, R. Judah and R. Shimon disagreed. The issue at stake concerned the following Biblical command: "You shall not take the widow's raiment in pledge" (*Deuteronomy 24:7*). When someone borrowed money it was customary for him to give his creditor some object as security. In the case of a poor person, who might well be short of articles to give for this purpose, it might often be that he would be forced to deposit some article of clothing. And to do so might be, for him, a real deprivation. Elsewhere in the same chapter the *Torah* makes a similar provision against causing the poor to suffer in this way:

And if he [the borrower] be a poor man, you shall not

sleep with his pledge. You shall surely restore the pledge to him when the sun goes down, that he may sleep in his garment, and bless you; and it shall be considered righteousness to you before the L-rd your G-d. [Deuteronomy 24:12-13]

Returning to the first case: the widow. Now in this case the Bible does not speak about whether she is poor or rich. Does the law apply to all widows or only to poor ones who needed the special economic protection? A *baraita* records the following:

A pledge may not be exacted from a widow whether she is poor or rich, as it is said: You shall not take the widow's raiment in pledge — this is the view of R. Judah. R. Shimon says: If she is rich, she is subject to distraint, but not if she is poor, for you are required to restore [the pledge] to her, and you thereby give her a bad reputation among her neighbors.

What does he mean? This is what he means: Since you exact a pledge from her, you are obliged to return it to her. And as a result of having to return it to her, you give her a bad reputation among her neighbors.
[Talmud, Baba Metzia 115a; Talmud, Sanhedrin 21a]

Thus, R. Judah holds that the law applies to all widows; R. Shimon holds that it applies only to poor widows. R. Shimon arrives at his conclusion in an interesting way. Not content to simply look at the words of the command, he goes further and penetrates to the *point* of the command. Why was it given? Because, says R. Shimon, there is another law that if the borrower is a poor person and has deposited something that he needs as a pledge, then the lender must return it to him every day or every night, so that he is not deprived of its use. Now, if the borrower is a widow, and she is visited every day by the lender who has to give back the pledge temporarily, this will cause her embarrassment because of what her neighbors might say. Now, concludes R. Shimon, since the purpose of the law was to spare her the risk of acquiring a bad reputation, it is obviously only relevant in the case of a poor widow. For if she is rich, then there is no obligation on the lender to restore the pledge daily, and indeed no necessity for him to even think of doing so.

The principle that R. Shimon uses here, and which is peculiarly associated with him, is *dorshin ta'amei dekra*; which roughly means that we restrict a Biblical command to the cases where its reason is relevant. It is the point of a command that determines its interpretation. And it is this principle that R. Judah opposes. For him, a command means what it says: no less and no more.

As we can see, it makes a real practical difference which view we take. And the issue between them is still argued today, outside Jewish circles, in the sphere of jurisprudence. Is a statute to be interpreted merely by looking at its wording, or are we to take into consideration the intentions of the legislators; that is, what end they were trying to achieve?

Again, it should not be hard to see that, despite the new context, it is ultimately the same argument as before. What is decisive? The facts or the intention? The facts are before us: the words of the *Torah*. And those words make no distinction between widows, poor or rich. But as always for R. Shimon, what counts is the intention. The intention of the command was to protect the feelings and the reputations of the widows. And this has bearing only upon poor widows. For rich ones will not have their creditors visiting them every day.

The unity of Israel

So far we have traced a particular facet of mysticism through its practical implications, in political attitudes, in the laws of *Shabbat*, and in the interpretation of the *Torah*. But for our final study of the attitudes of R. Shimon in contrast with those of R. Judah, we shall consider a far more dramatic case, a situation of acute moral dilemma. And to understand what lies behind it we must once again reconsider the mystical viewpoint.

For the mystic, what counts as reality is the inherent presence of the Infinite behind all the scattered phenomena of the world as we see it. But how can we have a conception of this invisible presence which gives life to everything and yet can never be seen? Yet there is an analogy: the relation of the human soul to the body.

We know that, in relation to ourselves, we present only a mere surface of our personality to the world. No one can see into ourselves as we can. What is this "self" or soul, the "I" that we refer to when we talk in the first person? We know it is not the body: our bodies change constantly, yet we remain the same person. It is not even our personality; that too may change. Though I may act and feel differently than I once did, I have not ceased to be me. To this self we give the name of "soul." It is the most mysterious of all phenomena. Despite attempts to identify it with the brain, it remains elusive and indefinable. Yet it is more familiar to us than anything else: through it we see the world and react to it as an individual quite distinct from anyone else.

The soul may hide its face even from its possessor. From Freud we learned to call this phenomenon the unconscious. That is, we may have motives that we hide even from our own conscious minds. But this was known long ago to the

Jewish mystics. It is just that they took a somewhat different view of what it was like: it was a *G-dly soul*. Deep down, without knowing it, every Jew longs to keep the *Torah* and come close to G-d with a love that burns like fire. The mystical task is to take a journey into the interior of the self, and rescue that love from its hiddenness.

The soul is infinite and intangible, yet in some way it inhabits the finite and tangible body. A paradox, certainly, but one with which we live. So, too, G-d, the Soul of the world, infinite and unperceivable though He is, inhabits the world, limited and physical though it is.

Just as the mystic, inwardly, tries to move ever closer to the roots of his soul, so, outwardly, he tries always to fathom the Infinite who gives life to the world.

But this is more than just an analogy. In several dazzling passages in the *Tanya*, the classic statement of *Chabad* thought, R. Schneur Zalman of Liadi spells out the reality behind the comparison. It is not simply that the soul in its relation to the body is like G-d in His relation to the world, but that every G-dly soul is literally a part of G-d. Man, at his most spiritual level, does more than relate to G-d: he contains part of the reality of G-d.

But G-d, as Maimonides lays down as one of the principles of the Jewish faith, is One and indivisible. How then can many souls each be a part of something that cannot be split or analyzed into parts? The truth is, at the deepest level, the entire community of Jewish souls is a single unity, standing in relation to one another as do the limbs of the body — many parts but a single entity. (see *Tanya*, especially chapter 2)

This again is no mere abstract doctrine. It has the most radical implications for our feelings and behavior. The *Torah* says, "You shall love your neighbor as yourself"

(*Leviticus 19:18*). No doubt this is easier said than done. But there are cases where love flows easily and naturally for most people: for instance, the love of a parent for his child. He loves his child because he stands in a special relationship to him; the parent has brought the child into being.

The radical conclusion of R. Schneur Zalman's mysticism is that, at the level of soul, every Jew is related to every other with complete identity. Between each Jew is a bond closer even than the closest we can speak of in non-mystical terminology, the bond between parent and child. "You shall love your neighbor as yourself" — *because he is yourself*. If we could attain this level of perception, then that love would flow unforced and without limits.

But how do we get there? This, too, is obvious. When we think of human beings as bodies, then certainly each is separate and distinct. It is only when we relate to ourselves and others at the level of the soul, can we begin to sense the unity. And hence the task of the mystic — and, in truth, the task of Judaism as a whole — is to move from body to soul; from reactions prompted by ordinary physical stimuli to those wholly spiritual in character and motivation. (*Tanya*, chapter 32)

The result? A profound emphasis on the love of every Jew, an emphasis that flows not simply from an emotion of benevolence but from a new way of viewing our identity and that of our fellow. And at the same time a simultaneous stress on two things that might, in any other context, seem incompatible: the infinite worth of the individual and the literal unity of the whole Jewish people. The individual, because he is a part of G-d and every fragment of infinity is infinite. The community, because, at the level of soul, there are no divisions that set person against person and create ultimate loneliness.

If Israel lacked one person

These are revolutionary ideas. Certainly, they are implicit in the *Torah*. But it takes a special cast of mind to uncover them. As we read through the early rabbinic literature we find that no one, to my knowledge, expounds this view so strongly as R. Shimon bar Yochai.

Consider the following passage, not attributed explicitly to him, but taken from the work that bears his name, the *Mechilta de-Rabbi Shimon bar Yochai*:

> *And you shall be to Me a kingdom of priests and a holy nation* [Exodus 19:6] — *this teaches that they are like a single body, a single soul. And thus it says: And who is like Your people Israel, a nation one in the earth* [II Samuel 7:23; I Chronicles 17:21]. *If one of them sins, they are all punished, as it is said: Did not Achan the son of Zerach commit a trespass concerning the devoted thing, and wrath fell upon all the congregation of Israel? And that man perished not alone in his iniquity* [Joshua 22:20]. *If one of them is smitten, they all feel pain.* [Mechilta de-Rabbi Shimon bar Yochai, to Exodus 19:6; edn. Epstein/Melamed p. 139]

A single body, a single soul. The proof? That when Achan, an individual, sinned, the entire nation suffered a defeat at Ai after their previous conquest of Jericho (see *Joshua* chapter 7). The corollary? That no Jew can be indifferent to the fate of others, for it is his fate, too.

The most famous image in which this was expressed belongs, also, to R. Shimon:

> *R. Shimon bar Yochai taught: It is to be compared to people who were in a boat, and one of them took a drill and began to drill a hole beneath himself. His*

> *companions said to him: Why are you doing this? He replied: What concern is it of yours? Am I not drilling under myself? They replied: But you will flood the boat for us all* [Midrash Rabbah, Leviticus 4:6].

The two sides of unity: an individual cannot harm himself without harming the whole of Israel; an individual cannot be content with self-perfection, ignoring the fate of the community.

The passage continues with what seems to be merely further proof of this idea, taken from the book of *Job*. In fact, it does more. It tells us something of the psychology of isolation:

> *And thus too did Job argue: And if it be indeed that I have erred, then my error remains with myself* [Job 19:4]. *But his companions said to him: When he adds to his sin, he attaches rebellion to us* [Job 34:37] — *you attach your iniquities to us* [Midrash Rabbah, Leviticus ibid.].

Job, sunk in the miseries of loss and despair, suffers a profound crisis of faith. When others try to comfort him Job, like the man who makes the hole in the boat, replies that it is none of their concern. But they insist; his fate is theirs, and they too will be held guilty.

This text is more than an example; it is a diagnosis. Depression, anxiety, melancholy, self-absorption and self-pity — these are both symptoms and causes of a loss of religious vision. R. Shimon seems to suggest that, if only Job would see that at the deepest level of self he is not an isolated individual, then he would not have lapsed into nihilism, would have been able to survive his acute personal tragedy, and would have avoided his religious crisis.

It is a point made again with added emphasis in *Tanya* (chapter 26), and stands at the furthest extreme from the philosophies of existential individualism that have dominated the intellectual life of the twentieth century. The lonely man, experiencing the angst of isolation and making his private choices in a world bereft of meaning: this archetype, admired by Sartre, Heidegger and others, is for R. Shimon spiritually empty.

But as we said before, in Jewish mysticism the very emphasis on the community is at the same time an insistence on the infinite worth of the individual. This again is in opposition to other ideologies of our time, such as Marx and others, which exalt collectivity at the expense of the individual. The clearest statement in which both ideas are brought together is in R. Shimon's description of the giving of the *Torah*:

> *R. Shimon bar Yochai said: From where do we learn that if a single person had been missing from Israel, the Divine Presence would not have appeared to them? Because it is written: For on the third day, the L-rd will come down in the sight of all the people upon Mount Sinai* [Exodus 19:11; Midrash Rabbah, Deuteronomy 7:8; see also Mechilta de-Rabbi Shimon bar Yochai and Mechilta de-Rabbi Ishmael to Exodus 19:11].

If one person is missing, then the whole community is incomplete and its full coming-together with the Divine Presence is impossible. It is an idea that was to be taken up with great force by later mysticism, in particular by the *ARI* — R. Isaac Luria — by the *Baal Shem Tov* and the *Chassidic* movement.

May one be sacrificed for the many?

The general implication follows immediately: love of fellow-man, active concern for the welfare of others, a refusal to tolerate isolationism, an equal refusal to sanction attitudes that lead to the dismissal of any individual as unworthy — the complex of approaches that have become the hallmark of *Chassidism*.

But we shall focus upon a specific implication, to show yet again that mysticism has practical applications that would not follow from other ways of thinking about Judaism. Again, the protagonists are R. Judah and R. Shimon. And this time the subject at issue is one of agonizing moral choice.

The Jews in Israel suffered severe persecutions at the hands of the Romans. Not only was the Temple destroyed, but in the aftermath there occurred the chilling events at Masada, when the Zealots decided to take their own lives rather than be killed by their enemies. Less than a century later, in the reprisals following the failure of the Bar Kochba uprising, persecution became a savage reality once more. Many of the greatest rabbis in Jewish history, R. Akiva the most famous of them all, went to their deaths as martyrs rather than give up their public teaching of *Torah*. It is against this backdrop that the following ruling, contained in the *Tosefta*, can be understood:

> *A company of men is confronted by non-Jews. They say: Give us one of your number whom we will kill. If you do not, we will kill all of you. Even though all of them will be killed, let them not deliver a single Jewish soul into their hands* [Tosefta, Terumot 7:23].

An almost impossible dilemma. We are to imagine

what was much more than a hypothetical possibility. A group of Jews is travelling on a journey (the *Talmud Yerushalmi*, in its citation of the *Tosefta*, adds the words "who were travelling on the road" — *Talmud Yerushalmi, Terumot 8:4*) when they are set upon by heathens intent upon blood. They issue an ultimatum: either hand one of yourselves over or we will kill everyone of you. The *halachic* ruling is simple, stark and uncompromising. There can be no compliance with their request. To hand over an innocent Jew to death is unforgivable in any circumstance. Even if they must all die as a result of their refusal, at least they will not have shared in the guilt.

In the whole rabbinic literature from then to the final codification, this particular ruling was never challenged, never the subject of argument, it gives us awe-inspiring insight into the supreme moral inflexibility of courage that the *Halachah* categorically demands.

However, there were cases — and again be aware that we are speaking about historical reality, not a theoretical discussion — that were similar in kind yet more complex in their ramifications. What happened when the situation was not an isolated one of meaningless violence, but an official one involving, say, the Roman authorities seeking someone regarded as a political subversive and who took refuge in a township?

Here, two new factors enter the equation. The first: the person sought is not just anyone; they know precisely whom they want. The burden of choosing does not fall upon the Jewish community. Second: on a scale, with such opponents as the Roman legions, and with whole townships at stake, there enters into the equation the question of the survival of the Jewish people as a whole. Already bereft of its Temple and its political independence, might some compromise be made to ensure that the entire nation not die as martyrs?

Now the moral issue becomes almost paralyzing. Legions surround a town and insist that a specific individual be handed over, and if not the entire town will be massacred. The mind is numbed by such a choice. Again we should pause to reflect that the rabbis did not recoil from this dilemma, concluding as they might have that any decision in such a circumstance would be wrong and that there is nothing that can be said. Instead, they brought to bear on it the same intellectual rigor and moral strength that they employed on every other issue, great or small.

This is the argument that ensued:

> R. Judah said: When are these words intended to apply? When he [the man sought] is inside and they [the Jewish community] are outside. But if he is inside and they are inside, since he would be killed and they would be killed, let them give him to them and let them not all be slain. And thus it is written: And the woman came to all the people in her wisdom [II Samuel 20:22] — which means she said to them: Since he would be killed and you would be killed, give him to them and you should not all be slain.
>
> R. Shimon said: This is what it means. She said to them: Anyone rebelling against the kingship of the house of David is deserving of death [Tosefta, Terumot, ibid; Midrash Rabbah, Genesis 94:9].

This is a difficult passage, and needs to be understood in stages.

What was R. Judah doing in the course of his cryptic remarks? He was, in fact, responding to the dilemma in the way in which a Jew is bound to do in cases where there is not already a clear-cut ruling in existence. He searched the *Torah* for a case that might serve as a precedent and give guidance in the present instance.

He found it in an episode that occurred during the reign of King David. There was an insurrection against the king:

> *And there happened to be there a worthless man whose name was Sheva ben Bichri, a Benjaminite; and he blew the* shofar *and said: We have no part in David, neither have we inheritance in the son of Yishay: every man to his tents, O Israel* [II Samuel 20:1].

Under the leadership of Yo'av, David's troops pursued Sheva, who eventually took refuge in the town of Avel. Yo'av's troops surrounded the town and were about to destroy it. A woman of the town conducted negotiations with Yo'av, who made it clear that the town would be spared if they would hand Sheva over to them. She reported the ultimatum to the townspeople. They agreed to the request, and Sheva met a bloody end. It is from this passage that R. Judah quotes.

Now here, on the face of it, was a precedent for some limited degree of compromise. The choice was the same: either hand over an individual or all die. And, in fact, they handed him over. What was the basis of their decision? R. Judah proceeds to reconstruct the argument that must have taken place, and the reasoning that the woman used to persuade her townspeople to hand over Sheva.

She must have argued thus, he says: either way Sheva will be killed. If he is handed over he will be killed. If the whole town is destroyed, he will be killed. The situation is hopeless. We cannot possibly survive the besieging troops outside the city walls. Therefore: since he will die in any case, rather let us not all die as well. For we would not thereby save him.

Having arrived at this point, R. Judah proceeds to his conclusion. If the Jewish community is "outside" — that is, they are not completely surrounded, they have some chance either of escaping or of defending themselves against total annihilation — then no compromise must be made. A Jewish soul must never be handed over if there is some alternative.

But if the community is "inside" with no means of escape, then — since they will all die anyway, and the wanted man with them — then rather they should hand him over than that they should all die.

This is a sober and sensitive response to the crisis. It dictates that the handing-over should be done only if there is absolutely no alternative. And it produced a compromise for extreme situations, which, would ensure that whole communities of Jews should not die at the hands of the enemy.

So far R. Judah. But not so R. Shimon. He rejects the analogy and with it the compromise. How, he says, can one cite a precedent from the case of Sheva ben Bichri? Sheva rebelled against the authority of a lawfully appointed king of Israel. And in Jewish law such insurrection warranted the death penalty. The people of Avel were correct in handling him over. And there was no need for calculations or fine moral distinctions.

Not so with the Romans. They are not the lawfully appointed kings of Israel. They are an occupying tyrannical power, who have destroyed the Temple, taken away our statehood, killed our Sages and teachers, and threatened those who publicly maintained the institutions of *Torah*. Nothing could be less akin to the rule of David.

Thus, the analogy fails. And with it disappears the

slightest grounds for ever collaborating with the requests of the enemy. Never is there an adequate reason to betray a soul of Israel and hand him over to death — even if a whole town must become martyrs to the cause of Jewish integrity. For R. Shimon there can be no justified compromise.

Here is idealism of a truly awesome order. And it is in character. For we have already seen that R. Shimon himself placed his life in danger by refusing to silence his feelings about the Roman conquerors.

The practical implication of infinity

Yet there is a question that calls out for an answer. Let us concede with R. Shimon that no analogy could be drawn from the case of Sheva ben Bichri. Yet surely R. Judah's argument, even shorn of its Biblical support, remains valid. If the wanted man will die, whether he be handed over or not, then rather let the community survive by delivering him up. For they will achieve nothing by their refusal. Is the logic of this point not unanswerable?

Only now do we begin to reach a full sense of the practical implications of infinity. Finitude is quantifiable, infinity is not. If human life is very precious, and yet still finite in its value, then there is a difference between one man dying and many. And this difference makes it sometimes — *in extremis* — justifiable to sacrifice the one for the sake of the many. To be sure, R. Judah did not accept this line of thinking in many cases: where the community might escape or fight back or where the request was for anyone, not for a named enemy of the besieging power. But he did accept it in one case. And this is the crux. For it implies that the death of many is worse than the death of one. And this implies that life is quantifiable. Again, let us be clear that R. Judah does not hold any of the doctrines, antithetical to the whole of Judaism, which hold that life is quantifiable against other things: suffering, or the happiness of others, or any other principle that would allow a life to be expendable under certain conditions. That is not his intention. Life cannot be measured against anything else. But it can, in the last analysis, be measured against other lives.

R. Shimon, as we have already seen, believes that each individual life is literally infinite. If one soul had been missing, the Israelites could not have received the *Torah*, could not have received the Divine Presence. And infinity cannot be quantified. Infinity times one and infinity times one hundred are the same. So devastating is the loss of a single life that the enormity is infinite. And as between the death of one and the death of many there can be no calculations. This total refusal to enter into any quantification where "one Jewish soul" is concerned is the strict consequence of taking infinity with absolute seriousness. No other point of view could have justified R. Shimon's conclusion. Nothing less than...his mysticism of the Jewish soul.

Once this refusal to calculate has been made, there remains just one question: to collaborate with tyrants or not? And to this there is only one answer.

A sequel

In a dilemma of this kind, it goes without saying that there is no one right answer. And the argument between R. Judah and R. Shimon is the sort of which it is said that "these and these are the words of the living G-d." Nonetheless, it might be thought that the unremitting idealism of

R. Shimon was, in this case, simply too much to be borne, and that his view was dismissed from the final elucidation of the law.

As it happens, it was not so. The argument had an interesting sequel. A century later, the *Talmud Yerushalmi* reports that a similar disagreement arose between the *amoraim*, R. Jochanan and Resh Lakish (*Talmud Yerushalmi, Terumot 8:4*). The terms had shifted somewhat. But broadly speaking, R. Jochanan favors compromise roughly on the terms of R. Judah, while Resh Lakish is nearly, though not quite, as extreme as R. Shimon. R. Jochanan says that the request to hand over should be met so long as it is for a named individual. Resh Lakish holds that it should only be met if that individual is "deserving of death like Sheva ben Bichri." It is difficult to be quite sure what Resh Lakish means. He cannot mean exactly what R. Shimon had meant, since R. Shimon's point was that Sheva ben Bichri had rebelled against a Jewish king, and therefore there was never a case where insurrection against a foreign tyranny was comparable. Had Resh Lakish meant this, then he would surely have said that no individual should ever be handed over. Presumably what he means is that sometimes, if rarely, the wanted man really has committed an act of great wickedness, which would be punished severely by Jewish law, if Jewish law were in force.

Resh Lakish's view is very much in the spirit of R. Shimon; and we know from other sources that R. Shimon's views left a deep impression upon him when he heard them from R. Jochanan his teacher (see, for example, *Talmud Berachot 31a*: "R. Jochanan said in the name of R. Shimon bar Yochai: It is forbidden for a man to fill his mouth with laughter in this world... It was related of Resh Lakish that he never again filled his mouth with laughter in this world

after he heard this saying from R. Jochanan his teacher.''
This particular insistence of R. Shimon was a measure of the
absolute seriousness with which he treated the fact of *Galut*:
see *Otzar HaGeonim* to *Berachot ad loc.*). So far, however,
we would have thought that the law followed R. Jochanan,
in accordance with the general rule that when teacher and
disciple disagree, the law is like the teacher. But the *Talmud
Yerushalmi* proceeds to relate an episode in which the issue
was put to the test; and it does so in terms which are by any
standard remarkable:

> *Ulla bar Koshev was sought by the [Roman] govern-
> ment. He fled to Lod, to the house of R. Joshua ben
> Levi. [Roman troops] came and surrounded the town.
> They said: If you do not hand him over we will
> destroy the town. R. Joshua ben Levi went up to him
> [Ulla], persuaded him [to submit], and handed him
> over. The prophet Elijah, of blessed memory, had
> been accustomed to reveal himself to R. Joshua ben
> Levi; but he stopped visiting him. R. Joshua fasted
> many fasts, and Elijah appeared again. [In answer to
> why he had stayed away, Elijah said:] Shall I reveal
> myself to betrayers? He replied: But have I not acted
> upon a rabbinic teaching? Elijah replied: Is this a
> teaching for pious men?* [Mishnat Chassidim]

The great Joshua ben Levi is censured by no less than
Elijah the prophet. The term used, "betrayer," is not a light
one. Such a person has no share in the World-To-Come
(*Maimonides, Hilchot Teshuvah 3:12*; see *Talmud, Baba
Metziah 83b*; *Talmud, Gittin 7a*; *RIF* to *Talmud, Baba
Kamma 117a*). And yet R. Joshua ben Levi had acted in
accordance with an accepted teaching. First, the Romans had
sought a specific named individual, so that the handing over

met the requirement of the *Tosefta* and of R. Jochanan. Secondly, there is no suggestion that Ulla bar Koshev was innocent; in which case even Resh Lakish would have agreed to the action. Indeed, Elijah does not dispute that the action was ultimately justifiable in terms of the *Halachah*. Yet, a pious man will simply not act this way.

What else should R. Joshua ben Levi have done? The commentators are perplexed (see the comments in the manuscript editions of *Hagahot Maimoniyot* to *Hilchot Yesodei HaTorah* 5:5; *responsum* of *Mar Rav Shalom Gaon*; *Meiri*; and *TAZ*, cited in *Sefer HaMada* of *Maimonides, ed. Lieberman, Mossad HaRav Kook, p. 116*. Compare also the text of the parallel passage in *Midrash Rabbah, Genesis* 94:9). Whatever the answer, it seems reasonable to suggest that while the *Halachah* follows Resh Lakish, Elijah was expressing the still stronger view of R. Shimon bar Yochai, which is that it is never right to hand over a Jew to the enemy, whatever the circumstances and whatever the consequences.

The *Halachah*, that is to say, follows the person closest to R. Shimon's extreme view, namely, Resh Lakish. And more than this: a *chassid*, a pious man, will not even avail himself of this narrow basis for compromise, but will stand firm by the ruling of R. Shimon, and urge others to do so. And indeed Maimonides codifies it. For having stated the law in terms equivalent to those of Resh Lakish, he adds the phrase "but we do not, *ab initio*, instruct people of this rule" (*ve-ein morin lahem kein lechatchilah, Hilchot Yesodei HaTorah* 5:5). This is his equivalent of the prophet Elijah's censure.

The spirit of R. Shimon bar Yochai's unremitting refusal to collaborate with tyranny, his refusal to enter into calculations that involved the quantifying of human lives, hangs heavily over the final verdict of the *Halachah*. Neither the compromise of R. Judah nor the later one of R. Jochanan was accepted.

Sometimes carrying a mystical vision through into real situations demands courage of a supernatural order. Such was R. Shimon's way. Yet sometimes just such a vision is closer to ultimate human realities than the more worldly, accommodating one of R. Judah. Moments of truth like this are thankfully rare. Yet it is our painful duty to recall that in this century, under the shadow of death of the Holocaust, the question was raised again, in yet more bitter terms. Jews were asked to collaborate with the Nazis in deciding which of their brothers should live and which should be handed over to death. The facts and the rabbinic responses are on record (see *Irving J. Rosenbaum*, The Holocaust and Halakhah, KTAV 1976, pp 24-31), and they should be read to gain a full sense of the tragic consequences of ever agreeing to collaborate with murderers, of ever moving away from the position of R. Shimon bar Yochai.

An old man's lesson

Our purpose was to show that mysticism makes a difference; that infinity has practical implications. And to do so we have followed the footsteps of R. Shimon bar Yochai through politics, the laws of *Shabbat*, methods in interpreting the *Torah*, attitudes towards the individual and the community, and finally an extreme crisis in moral decision-making. In each case R. Shimon's vision did make a difference, and he was faithful to the inferences to be drawn from his original perception.

We have met a man whose idealism and uncompromising character seem almost impossible to approach. Is it possible to live by the standards of R. Shimon? On one point, at least, the *Talmud* asks just this question: on the issue of how to compromise between the demands of learning *Torah* day and night, and the necessity of working for a livelihood. By now we will already have guessed what R. Shimon's response would be: no compromise. Learn *Torah*. He had no time for the solution of his contemporary, R. Ishmael — that learning *Torah* should be combined with a worldly occupation — nor even for that of R. Judah, that the two should be combined but that study should take first place. The *Talmud* records the sad but resigned verdict of Abaye: "Many followed the advice of R. Ishmael and it has worked well; others have followed R. Shimon bar Yochai, and it has not been successful" [*Talmud, Berachot 35b*].

But it is precisely this that gives us a measure of re-assurance. For it seems that R. Shimon was censured by Heaven for being too other-worldly after his long seclusion in the cave, hidden from everyday life and its problems. He was, records the *Talmud*, sent back to the cave for another twelve months to learn the lesson [*Talmud, Shabbat 33b*]. In the end, it seems, he was not *too* mystical, but rather not mystical enough. For he had yet to learn the *infinite significance of ordinary things* and of *ordinary people*: that the fire of the love of G-d can be seen in the face of each Jew, when one has learned to see into the soul.

R. Shimon was eventually taught this lesson by an ordinary Jew. And perhaps it was the deepest message of all. This is what happened when Rabbi Shimon and his son finally emerged from their seclusion:

> On the eve of Shabbat, *before sunset, they saw an old man holding two bundles of myrtle and running at*

twilight. *"What are they for?"* they asked him. *"They are in honor of the* Shabbat.*"* *"But,"* they asked, *"surely one should be sufficient?"* He replied, *"One is for the command of 'Remember' and one is for the command of 'Observe.'"*

Then R. Shimon said to his son: *"See how precious are the commandments to Israel."* And their minds were set at rest. [Talmud, Shabbat 33b]

Jewish Value Systems

Dr. Yitzchak Block

You can learn more about a person from his unguarded moments than from watching him when he knows that he is the center of your attention. Similarly, we can learn more about a culture or a society from its off-hand customs than we can from its established philosophy. I propose to call your attention to a few off-hand customs in Western society and comment on them in a manner that is significant when one compares these with the Jewish attitude to the same things. If I am not mistaken, one can find a fundamental difference between the value systems of the Western World and that of the *Torah* way of life.

In our society, removal of the hat is a sign of respect. One enters a home, a place of worship, or comes before the Queen bareheaded. The reverse is so with the Jew. Covering the head is a sign of respect. Thus it is forbidden to mention G-d's name with one's head uncovered. The *Shulchan Aruch* states that it is the mark of a pious man that he keeps his head covered at all times. In our day, the wearing of the *kipah* has become the *sine qua non* of the religious Jew. If you wish, it has become his uniform. Perhaps this is so for the very reason that it noticeably contrasts with the way of the world around us. This difference of practice is a symptom of a more deep-seated divergence in values.

The covering of the head is meant as a constant reminder that there is a power higher than human reason or understanding. Even though man's reason be that which renders him pre-eminent among other creatures and makes him "divine" as some philosophers have said, nonetheless, the *Torah* proclaims that this is not man's greatest or most valuable capacity and, Aristotle notwithstanding, man's reason is not what makes him divine. The highest power in man is the recognition of the Creator as a Being who utterly transcends reason, whom we call G-d and before whom man is duty-bound to make his reason subservient and to humble himself. This is the ultimate truth of man's situation in the world. It is not only a metaphysical truth, it is a moral one as well. This may sound like heresy to modern man. After all, it is man's reason that has enabled him to make such great strides in science and that has ushered in a new age of control and understanding of nature. This has come about through the free inquiry of the human mind unfettered by dogma or tradition. There lies buried in this apparent contradiction between science and *Torah* a confusion that is just beginning to become clear in our own day.

The free inquiry of science does not pursue a truth that can in some sense displace the truth of G-d. Science has come to see that it cannot unfold the truth or the ultimate reality of nature. Science can give us a glimpse into the workings of nature and control over its forces. But science and technology cannot ensure the moral well-being of man. As we have see so clearly in our own day, the nation that stood in the forefront of science and technology utilized its knowledge to bring the most wanton and cruel destruction of life and property the world had known until that time. In our own day, the fact that we possess great scientific knowledge and can perform astounding feats of space-flight and the like in no way ensures that we shall use this skill for good rather than evil.

It is a fallacy to suppose that the morality and well-being of man advances with the progress of science or the advancement of knowledge. This fallacy is a legacy from Plato who proclaimed that knowledge itself is virtue and thus the highest form of knowledge leads to the highest virtue. For Plato the highest form of knowledge was geometry and it would seem to follow that geometers are the most virtuous of men. The falsity of this requires no comment. Nor is this fallacy alleviated by replacing geometry with nuclear physics or even philosophy. In fact, the word "virtue" has almost disappeared from the vocabulary of moral philosophy. One need only peruse publishers' advertisements of books on moral philosophy to see that the latest fashion in moral philosophy is to argue for the acceptance not only of abortion (which is already accepted tradition) but homosexuality, infanticide, euthanasia, sodomy and even incest.

If I were speaking to a philosophical audience I could not assume that they would be shocked by such advertisements and all that they imply. I would have to present an argument that could rationally demonstrate why adultery, sodomy and even incest are morally evil, and frankly, I know of no such argument. If your ethical consciousness is shocked by such an advertisement, the reason is that whether you keep *Shabbat* or don *tefillin* every day, you are still close enough to your heritage as a Jew to feel within your bones the moral repugnance of such acts, which controvert the *Torah's* definition of the sanctity of the Jewish People. Our

Torah defines the sanctity of the Jewish people: "...you shall not commit any of these abominations (homosexuality, sodomy and incest referred to above), neither the homeborn nor the stranger in your midst — for all these abominations have been done by the people of the land before you and they have defiled the land — that the land not spew you out when you defile it as it has spewed out the nations which were before you," "...holy you shall be; for I the L-rd your G-d am holy" (*Leviticus 18:26-28, 19:2*). I used to think when I read this passage how really debased one must be in order for such things to have an appeal. In any event, I thought these things may have been common in primitive societies but were certainly not applicable to modern times. Suddenly this admonition seems uncommonly pertinent and up-to-date. Not only are such things commonplace but philosophers lend their dialectical skills to defend them.

Amongst the acts that are defended on grounds similar to the ones mentioned above are infanticide and euthanasia. What decides whether the infant or the infirm is allowed to live or die is an illusive factor called by doctors and bio-medical practitioners "quality of life." No one has yet defined "quality of life," but it is a code-word for enjoyment. As long as life has the prospect of enjoyment it is worthwhile, otherwise life is not worth the money and effort to foster or sustain it. This kind of philosophy seems rather benign at first glance, but it undermines a notion that is central to *Torah* and to the moral outlook on human life generally. That is, human life has a worth or value in itself, quite apart from its quality or whether one is happy or enjoying oneself. This is sometimes expressed by saying that human life is sacred, and that it enjoys a moral status that nothing else in the world enjoys. Its very existence is sacrosanct. This derives from the idea in the *Torah* that man was made in the image of G-d. There is a bit of G-d in every human being and this is why human life requires that it be treated with dignity and respect. It is this respect for the sanctity of life that is undermined by all arguments supporting infanticide and euthanasia. It is no accident that the technicians that Himmler sent to establish the first gas chambers and crematoria in which Jews were murdered were those who had built and maintained the Nazi euthanasia project that was initiated in 1939. Euthanasia and genocide are cousins. They derive from a common origin and philosophical outlook which is a denial of the sanctity of life.

The general philosophical position that lies behind most moral thinking today, some examples of which we have barely touched upon, goes under the rubric of "utilitarianism." Utilitarianism is unquestionably the most popular and forceful ethical theory today. It is so taken for granted that any attempt to challenge it is greeted with ridicule and scorn by most philosophers. In simple terms the theory says that what is morally good gives pleasure and moral evil is what causes pain or misery. This is what is really behind arguments that defend abortion, sodomy, incest, infanticide and euthanasia.

When Jeremy Bentham first propounded his theory of utilitarianism in the early part of the nineteenth century he had no idea that his theory would be used to defend the kinds of acts mentioned above which he would have considered truly evil. Himself a British M.P., Bentham originally intended his theory as a guide to legislators in fashioning laws that should try to make everyone as happy as possible rather than catering to a select few. No doubt this is a worthy motivation, but it renders the reason of man subservient to desire. If we are good men, we have good desires and all is well. If our desires are egotistical, avaricious and narcissistic as are the desires of most of us, then it is possible that our reason can serve as a tool for evil and we become: *chachomim hemoh lehorah (Jeremiah 4:22)* — men who utilize their understanding to serve their evil designs. Notice that utilitarianism so defines what is good as to exclude the possibility of there being such a thing as an evil pleasure or desire, for the good is stipulated to be whatever gives one pleasure, as long as one's pleasures do not cause pain and misery to others. Thus, according to utilitarianism, there is no such thing as pursuing a pleasure that is bad. The falsity of this position is attested to by anyone who has ever felt himself drawn to desires that he knows at the time are bad. Certainly I have experienced this and I would assume that many of you have, too. Sometimes we have the power to overcome them and sometimes we do not. Giving in to such desires creates disharmony and disturbance within ourselves and between ourselves and others. This in itself is a sign of evil — the creation of disharmony.

At this point the *Torah* steps into the picture and bids that we humble not only our minds but also our power of desire before G-d, and this in turn brings an inner harmony into the life of the person. The oneness of G-d attests to the oneness of the world and also of man. The essence of man, the world and G-d is oneness and the cement of this unity is love. The contradiction to this is the ego of man and its desires, which man's reason struggles to control.

There is a story told in the *Talmud* that before the famous sage Rabbi Nachman was born, a fortune-teller told his mother that her unborn child would grow up to be a thief. The distraught woman went to the *Bet Hamedrash* to inquire of the Rabbis what she should do. They advised her that from the moment her child was born, she should be scrupulous to see that his head was constantly covered. So she did and her son became the Rabbi instead of a thief. One day, the story continues, Rabbi Nachman was walking in the street and the wind blew his headgear off his head. Immediately, he was seized by a desire to steal which persisted until he replaced it. The power of the recognition of G-d and our subservience to Him can neutralize the instinctive desires that one might consider uncontrollable. This is the power that the *kipah* gives the Jew. The covering of the head is thus a fitting symbol that distinguishes the Jew in a society where acting on desire and pursuit of pleasure defines the meaning and value of life.

This story of Rabbi Nachman can instructively be compared with one about Jeremy Bentham, *l'havdil*, the founder of utilitarianism. Bentham endowed the University of London on the condition that his portly body be embalmed and hung in a glass case over the entrance to the University and there you can see it today. Bentham thought this would ensure eternal gratitude and respect. What it has earned him is derision, I think.

I recently heard a radio program in the U.S. in which the successor to the Ripley's Believe-It-Or-Not stories was asked which of all the weird and unbelievable stories he had collected from his travels over the world had he found the strangest and most unbelievable. He answered that there was some man (he didn't mention his name or that he was the founder of the most predominant school of moral philosophy today) in England who endowed the University of London on the condition that his embalmed body be placed over the entrance. This radio interview revealed an aspect of the story which I had not previously known. The benefactor's body had to be present at all board meetings and deference paid to it by a salute of some sort at the beginning of each meeting. The radio announcer's comment was that the story is revolting, and indeed it is. However, it is not much more revolting than some of the things now being defended by philosophers on the basis of utilitarianism as an ethical theory, things which Bentham in his day would have considered just as revolting. Nonetheless there is a consistent line of development from a game of pushpin (a game mentioned by Bentham) being good because it is pleasurable and sodomy being good because it is pleasurable. In either case the "head is uncovered" — the ego and the body reign supreme and it is a fitting memorial to this system of values that it is crowned with Bentham's portly body hovering over the heads of those who conduct the daily business of the pursuit of knowledge and understanding at one of England's most prestigious universities. All this acquisition of knowledge, when it is distilled into a way of life that is lived and defended by its practitioners, is far from what one would call a life of moral virtue or goodness.

How different from the image we have of the *talmud chacham* where wisdom and understanding is traditionally associated with humility. Their standard is *Moshe Rabbenu* who, though the greatest mortal who ever lived ("There arose no prophet ever again in Israel like Moses whom G-d knew face to face" [*Deuteronomy 34:10*]), was also the humblest of men: "And the man Moses was very humble more than any other man on the face of the earth" (*Numbers 12:3*). How are these contradictions merged into a harmony — greatness on the one hand and humility on the other? The answer to this question is that a Jew covers his head.

There are two more customs I would like to note here. In the world of Western fashion, men button their garments left over right. The origin of this custom, I am told, was to make access to weapons easier. When you meet a stranger be on guard and have your weapon ready. To ensure that you bear no malice stretch forth your right hand and shake to show you conceal no weapon. Jews have no fear of this. Our garments are traditionally buttoned right over left because we bear no weapons and when we meet we need not show that our hands are empty. Instead, we say: "*Shalom*" — peace! The *Kabbalah* says that the right side of a person should always take precedence over the left, for the right side of man signifies kindness while the left signifies sternness, justice and retribution. Just as G-d created the world primarily out of love and kindness (*Olam chesed yiboneh*), so love and kindness should predominate in men's dealings with one another. Therefore one buttons the right over the left even though this may hamper the drawing of a weapon.

A third and final custom: in Western society, when men drink together and toast one another, they clink their glasses. This is a throwback to the time when men, suspicious of one another, would not drink unless they poured some from each glass into every other for fear of poisoning. Jews have no fear of this when they drink together. They simply say: "*l'chaim*" — to life!

There is a connection between all these practices. The pride and egoism of man is that which sets the hand of one man or nation against another. It is the root of violence and destruction. It is what brings divisiveness to the life of man and destruction to the world.

One needs no philosophical argument to show that this is bad. And deep down *everyone* knows that harmony and unity are good. The ultimate source of harmony and unity is G-d, whom we Jews were the first to proclaim as truly One, in number and in the sense that everything ultimately is one and unified with G-d. Man, the world and G-d compose a harmonious unity that transcends the external divisiveness of these three things. The goal of *Torah* is to reveal this hidden unity. This is the ultimate good and the cement of this unity is love: love of our fellow, love for the world and love of G-d.

Man is a microcosm that contains within himself a miniature world where the forces of evil and good contend with one another for control of the mind and heart. The ego of man causes him to love himself, but man is commanded to love G-d with a love that is all-inclusive. As it says: "... you shall love G-d with all your heart...," leaving no room for self-love. Self-love which is the primordial instinct in man must be sublimated before the love of G-d. Then one can come to the essence of what *Torah* is all about, as Hillel told the heathen who wanted to learn the essence of *Torah* while standing on one foot: "Love your fellow like yourself." Underlying this cryptic and, on the surface, impossible injunction is the mysterious unity that underlies all things. We must love one another because in the final analysis we are one, and self-love and love of one's fellow at this level do merge and become indistinguishable.

This ideal is the end of a long and arduous journey or, should I say, exile, which began when G-d supplied all the Jewish people with one enormous *kipah*. He picked up Mt. Sinai and threatened to drop it on top of them if they would not receive His *Torah*. All the other nations excused themselves when it was offered them. It did not fit in with their way of doing things or their fashion or mode. Above all it did not seem rational to accept a commitment before one knew what one was committing oneself to. Indeed, it is not rational, and yet this is what G-d demanded — the surrender of one's will. He demanded that Jews cover their heads, their bodies, their egos. How our ancestors summoned up the ultimate trust in G-d required for this kind of commitment I do not know. But, we, standing more than thirty-two hundred years down the road from that great event, have it distilled into our bones by that many years of a history forged with sacrifice and faith. The struggle continues in modern terms with which we are all familiar and which each of us in our own way could document from our personal lives, whether we be university professors, businessmen or just plain *Chabadniks*. For me, however, the essence of this struggle is captured by the now-familiar figure of the soldier at the Wall praying — his head covered.

The Dynamics of Teshuvah

—————————— Rabbi Dr. J. Immanuel Schochet

> *"Rebbe, I am a sinner. I would like to return, to do teshuvah!"*
>
> *R. Israel of Ryzhin looked at the man before him. He did not understand what the man wanted:*
>
> *"So why don't you do teshuvah?"*
>
> *"Rebbe, I do not know how!"*
>
> *R. Israel retorted:*
>
> *"How did you know to sin?"*
>
> *The remorseful sinner answered simply:*
>
> *"I acted, and then I realized that I had sinned."*
>
> *"Well," said the Rebbe, "the same applies to teshuvah: repent and the rest will follow of itself!"*

Torah: The Ground Rules

Revelation is the foundation of religion. Revelation constitutes the basic premises of religion: (a) There is the Revealer. G-d exists. He is real. (b) G-d speaks to man. G-d not only exists, He also cares. He is a personal G-d. There is *hashgachah* (Divine Providence). Because G-d cares, like a loving and concerned parent cares for his child, He reveals to us what we should know about reality. He guides us and teaches us the way wherein we are to walk and the acts that we must do.

This is *Torah*, the "Tree of Life to those who hold fast to it."[1] G-d's word, the Revelation, is called *Torah*. For *Torah* means instruction: "It instructs and reveals that which was hidden, unknown."[2] "It teaches man to walk in the right path. It counsels him how to return to his Master."[3]

Revelation, the *Torah* in all its immensity of 248 commandments and 365 prohibitions, is realistic. It is not alien to man and physical reality. It is not superimposed from without. "It is not hidden from you nor far off. It is not in the heavens that you should say: Who shall go up for us to the heavens...? Neither is it beyond the sea that you should say: Who shall go over the sea for us...? It is very close to you, in your mouth and in your heart that you may do it."[4]

Torah is not attached to the world. It precedes and transcends the world.[5] It is the blueprint for Creation.[6] "The Holy One, blessed be He, looked into the *Torah* and created the world."[7]

The universe, man, all that exists, was created, fashioned and made on the basis of, and suited to, the contents and requirements of *Torah*. This allows for the possibility, and thus the demand, that man — every one of us — can live up to the obligations and ideals of *Torah*.[8]

We are bound up with *Torah* in a reciprocal relationship. As *Torah* is the blueprint for the universe, the universe reflects all components of *Torah*.[9] And as it is with the macrocosm, so it is with the microcosm, with man: The human body and the human soul reflect the 613 precepts: 248 organs corresponding to the 248 commandments; 365 veins corresponding to the 365 prohibitions.[10]

Observance of the positive precepts animates the relative organs, attaches them to Divinity and elicits for them Divine illumination, vitality and energy.[11] Observance of the prohibitions protects the relative veins and vessels against contamination, against influences alien to their nature and purpose.[12]

The Nature of Sin

Revelation, *Torah*, the life based upon it, constitutes morality, virtue, goodness.

What constitutes sin?

On the simple level, sin means breaking the law, violating the *Torah* by acts of omission or commission. Our duties are spelled out clearly. The law is defined. To ignore the letter or the spirit of the law, let alone to contravene it, that is sin.

On a deeper level, the meaning of sin is indicated in its Hebrew terminology. The general term for it is *aveirah*. It is of the root *avar* — to pass or cross over, to pass beyond. *Aveirah* means a trespass, a transgression, a stepping across the limits and boundaries of propriety to the "other side."

More specific words are *chet*, *avon*, *pesha*. *Chet* is of a root meaning to miss, to bear a loss. *Avon* is of a root meaning to bend, twist, pervert. *Pesha* is of a root meaning to rebel. Technically, legalistically, *chet* refers to inadvertent sins; *avon* to conscious misdeeds; and *pesha* to malicious acts of rebellion.[13]

Sin, thus, is a move away from Divinity, away from

truth. "Your sins separate you from your G-d"[14] who is truly "your life."[15] It separates us from *Torah*, our lifeline, that which attaches us to the source of our life and all blessings.

To neglect the commandments is to deprive ourselves of the illumination and vitality which their observance draws upon us, to forfeit an opportunity, to render ourselves deficient: *chata'im*, at a loss. To violate the prohibitions is to defile the body, to blemish the soul, to cause evil to become attached.[16]

Sin offers man temporary gains, but it is altogether irrational, self-defeating. Attractive and sweet at the outset, but bitter in the end.[17] Thus, "The Holy One, blessed be He, and the *Torah* are astounded: How is it possible that a person will sin?!"[18]

No person will commit a sin unless a spirit of folly has entered into him.[19] Sin is an act of ignorance or foolishness. Invariably it can be traced to lack of knowledge, to negligence or carelessness. If premeditated, let alone an act of willful rebellion, it is outright stupidity. Either way, it is rooted in heedlessness, in shortsightedness, in failure to think. It follows upon a blinding obsession with the here and now, egocentricity, self-righteousness.[20]

The Principle of Teshuvah

The folly of sin derives from man's physical nature. What is man? A composite of body and soul.

The soul is spiritual. By its very nature it reaches out to, and strives for, spirituality.

The body is material, and thus attracted to the allurements of its own elements, of matter.[21]

Yet these two are combined. The soul is removed from its "supernal peak" to be vested in the lowly body.

This "descent" is for the purpose of an "ascent": to elevate and sublimate the physicality of the body and the matter to which it is related in its lifetime.[22] There is tension between body and soul, between matter (and the natural or animalistic life-force that animates and sustains it), and the *neshamah*, the sublime soul and spirit of man. But they are not irreconcilable.

The body *per se* is neither evil nor impure. It is potentiality: not-yet-holy, even as it is not-yet-profane. Man's actions, the actions and behavior of the body-soul compound, determine its fall into the chambers of defilement or its ascent to be absorbed in holiness.[23]

To succeed in elevating and sublimating the body and its share in this world is an elevation for the soul as well. It is precisely the exposure to temptation, the risks of worldliness, the possibility of alternatives and the incumbent free will of man, that allow for achievement, for ultimate self-realization.[24]

"The body of man is a wick, and the light (soul) is kindled above it.... The light on a man's head must have oil, that is, good deeds."[25]

The wick by itself is useless if not lit. The flame cannot burn in a vacuum; it cannot produce light nor cling to the wick without oil. *Torah* and *mitzvot*, good deeds, unite the wick and the flame, the body and the soul, to actualize inherent potentiality, to produce a meaningful entity.[26]

The *neshamah*, the soul, a spark of G-dliness within us, fills us with practically unlimited potential. Man is granted the power to make of himself whatever he likes, in effect to determine his destiny.[27]

The veracity of mundane temptation, however, is no less real. "Sin crouches at the door."[28]

Torah confronts this fact: "There is no man so righteous on earth that he does good and never sins."[29]

If sin was final, the history of mankind would have begun and ended with Adam. The Creator took this into account. The original intent was to create the world on the basis of strict justice. As G-d foresaw that such a world could not endure, He caused the attribute of mercy to precede the attribute of justice and allied them.[30]

"When the Holy One, blessed be He, created the world, He consulted the *Torah* about creating man. She said to Him: 'The man You want to create will sin before You, he will provoke You to anger. If you will deal with him commensurate to his deeds, neither the world nor man will be able to exist before you!' G-d then replied to the *Torah*: 'Is it for nothing that I am called the Compassionate and Gracious G-d, long-suffering...?'"[31]

Thus, before creating the world, the Holy One, blessed be He, created *teshuvah* (repentance), and said to it: "I am about to create man in the world, but on condition that when they turn to you because of their sins, you shall be ready to erase their sins and to atone for them!"

Teshuvah thus is forever close at hand, and when man returns from his sins, this *teshuvah* returns to the Holy One, blessed be He, and He atones for all — all judgments are suppressed and sweetened, and man is purified from his sins. How is he purified from his sins? When he ascends with this *teshuvah* as he should. Rabbi Isaac said: When he returns before the Supreme King and prays from the depths of his heart, as it is written:[32] "From the depths I call unto You, the Eternal."[33]

Torah, the rules and regulations for life, preceded the

world and served as its blueprint. These rules demand strict adherence. "But for the *Torah*, heaven and earth cannot endure, as it is said:[34] 'If not for My covenant by day and by night, I had not appointed the ordinances of heaven and earth.' "[35]

Sin means to defeat the purpose of Creation, to deprive creation of all meaning. This must result in the world's reversion to nothingness. Thus the need for the attribute of mercy, of compassion.[36]

Mercy means to recognize the legitimacy of justice, yet to show compassion, to forgive nonetheless.[37] Mercy means to recognize the valid demands of the law, but also to temper these demands by considering the fact that "the drive of man's heart is evil yet from his youth."[38] It offers another chance.

This is the principle of *teshuvah*.

The Power of Teshuvah

> As for the wicked man, if he should return from all his sins that he committed and guard all my decrees, and do justice and righteousness, he shall surely live, he shall not die. All his transgressions which he committed will not be remembered against him.... Do I then desire the death of the wicked, says the Lord, the Eternal G-d, is it not rather his return from his ways, that he may live?
>
> Ezekiel 18[39]

"*Teshuvah* is a principle indispensable to religion, indispensable to the existence of individuals believing in the *Torah*. For it is impossible for man not to sin and err —

either by erroneously adopting an opinion or moral quality which in truth are not commendable, or else by being overcome by passion and anger. If man were to believe that this fracture can never be remedied, he would persist in his error and perhaps even add to his disobedience.

"The belief in *teshuvah*, however, leads him to improvement, to come to a state that is better, nearer to perfection than that which obtained before he sinned. That is why the *Torah* prescribes many actions that are meant to establish this correct and very useful principle of *teshuvah*."[40]

Without *teshuvah* the world could not endure. Without *teshuvah* man could not but despair, crushed by the burden of his errors. *Torah* is the foundation of the universe, it assures and sustains its existence. *Teshuvah* insures its survival.

The power of *teshuvah* is overawing. There is absolutely nothing that stands in the way of *teshuvah*.[41] The thread of *teshuvah* is woven throughout the whole tapestry of *Torah*, of our tradition.[42] It is not simply a *mitzvah*, one of 613 channels to tie us to G-d. It is a general, all-comprehensive principle, the backbone of religion.[43]

There is no sin that cannot be mended and remedied by *teshuvah*.[44] *Teshuvah* removes a burdensome past and opens the door to a new future. It means renewal, rebirth. The *ba'al teshuvah* becomes a different, a new, person.[45] It is much more than correction, more than rectification. *Teshuvah* elevates to a status even higher than the one prior to all sin. Even the perfectly righteous are surpassed by the *ba'al teshuvah*.[46]

Sin is time-consuming. It is an evolutionary process. Man does not fall at once, suddenly. He is trapped by one wrong act or attitude, often seemingly innocuous, which leads to another. When failing to recognize and stop this process, a chain-reaction is set into motion and leads to the mire of evil.[47]

Teshuvah, however, even in the worst of cases, is immediate. "*Ba'alei teshuvah* are meritorious. For in the span of... one instant they draw close to the Holy One, blessed be He, more so than the perfectly righteous who draw near... over the span of many years!"[48]

As *teshuvah* is not part of a gradual process and development, it is not subject to any order, to the "bureaucracy" of a normative procedure. It is a jump, a leap. A momentary decision to tear oneself away. One turn. One thought. And thus it affects even law, justice: When someone betrothes a woman on condition that "I am a *tzaddik*, a righteous person without sin," the betrothal is valid and binding even if he was known to be absolutely wicked. How so? Because at that very moment of proposal he may have meditated *teshuvah* in his mind![49]

The single thought, the momentary meditation of *teshuvah*, is sufficient to move man from the greatest depths to the greatest heights.

Just one thought, indeed; for the essence of *teshuvah* is in the mind, in the heart.[50] It is a mental decision, an act of consciousness, awareness, commitment.

The Nature of Teshuvah

Where does this enormous potency of *teshuvah* come from? How can it erase the past, change the present, mold the future — recreate, as it were?

The power of *teshuvah* derives from its transcendent nature. Like *Torah*, *teshuvah* preceded the Creation.[51] It is not part of the world, of Creation, of a creative process. It is beyond time, beyond space, rooted in infinity. In the sphere of infinity, past and present fade into oblivion.

Teshuvah is in the heart, in the mind.[50] One thought of *teshuvah* is enough. For thought, the mind, is not restricted by the limitations of the body. The mind can traverse the universe in seconds.[52] And the mind — *machshavah*, thought — is man, the essence of man.[53] Man is where his thoughts are.[54]

Fasting, self-mortification, may be means through which man expresses remorse. They may be acts of purification, of self-cleansing. But they do not constitute *teshuvah*.[55] *Teshuvat hamishkal*, penance commensurate to the sin, "to balance the scales," is important. So is *teshuvat hageder*, the voluntary erection of protective "fences" to avoid trespassing. Empirical reality may dictate such modes of behavior corresponding to certain forms of weakness.[56] However, these deal with symptoms only. They relate to specific acts that constitute the external manifestation of sin. They do not touch sin itself. They do not tackle the root and source from which sin grows. That root and source is in the mind, in the heart: Ignorance, carelessness, neglect, wrong attitudes, egocentricity, self-justification.

Just as sin is rooted in man's will and mind, so must *teshuvah* be rooted in man's will and mind.[57]

"He who sets his heart on becoming purified (from ritual defilement) becomes pure as soon as he has immersed himself (in the waters of a *mikvah*), though nothing new has befallen his body. So, too, it is with one who sets his heart on cleansing himself from the impurities that beset man's soul; namely, wrongful thoughts and false convictions: as soon as he consents in his heart to withdraw from those counsels and brings his soul into the waters of reason, he is pure."[58]

The tragedy of sin is not so much the transgression itself, to succumb to temptation, for "there is no man on earth... that he never sins." The real tragedy, the ultimate sin, is the failure to judge oneself, the failure to do *teshuvah*, "he has left off to contemplate to do good... he does not abhor evil."[59]

Better one self-reproach in the heart of man than numerous lashings.[60] As the bacteria, poisonous and infectious, are eliminated, their symptoms and outgrowths will disappear as well.[61] And as sins cease, sinners will be no more.[62] Thus *teshuvah*, the *teshuvah* that deals with the essence of sin, brings healing into the world.[63]

This is not to understate the external symptoms of sin. For with every transgression "man acquires a *kateigar*, a prosecutor, against himself."[64] The act of sin assumes reality. It clings to man, it attaches itself to him[65] — leading him further astray in this world only to accuse him later in the hereafter.[66]

On the other hand, everything in Creation is categorized in terms of matter and form (body and soul). The act of sin, its external manifestation, is the matter (the body) of sin, which creates the *kateigar*. The underlying thought, the intent, the will or passion that generated the transgression is the form (the soul) that animates and sustains that body.[67]

Self-mortification attacks that body and may destroy that matter. But only a change of heart, conscious remorse, is able to confront its form, its soul. Only the elimination of the thought, intent and desire that caused the sin will eliminate the soul of the *kateigar*. And when deprived of its soul, the *kateigar* ceases to exist.[68]

Thus "rend your heart and not your garments, and return unto the Eternal your G-d, for He is gracious and compassionate, long-suffering and abounding in kind-

ness...."[69] When rending the heart in *teshuvah*, there is no
need to rend one's garments.[70]

The Disposition of the Ba'al Teshuvah

Teshuvah is essentially in the heart, in the mind. It is
related to the faculty of *binah*, understanding.[71]

There cannot be *teshuvah* without a consciousness of
reality: understanding what is required. Recognition of one's
status. Introspection. Searing soul-searching. Honest self-
evaluation that opens the eyes of the mind and causes a
profound sense of embarrassment: How could I have acted
so foolishly? How could I have been so blind and dumb in
the face of the Almighty, the Omnipresent "Who in His
goodness renews each day, continuously, the work of Creation?"[72] How could I forsake the Ultimate, the Absolute,
for some transient illusion? "My people have committed
two evils: they have forsaken Me, the Fountain of Living
Waters, to hew for themselves cisterns, broken cisterns that
hold no water!"[73]

Teshuvah is directly related to *bushah* — shame,
embarrassment. The Hebrew word *teshuvah* contains the
letters of *boshet*; transposing the letters of *shuvah* (return),
offers the word *bushah* (shame). For *bushah* is an indication
of *teshuvah*.[74]

Bushah, a sense of shame, flows from an illuminating
grasp of reality. It is the proof of true regret over, and of a
break with, the past. It is identical with *teshuvah*. To
achieve that level is assurance of forgiveness: He who commits a sin and is ashamed of it, all his sins are forgiven him![75]

It takes understanding to do *teshuvah*: "His heart shall

understand, and he will return, and it shall be healed for him."[76] That is why first we pray: "bestow upon us wisdom, understanding and knowledge," and only then: "bring us back to You in complete *teshuvah*."[77]

Wisdom, understanding, knowledge, are prerequisites for *teshuvah*. It takes knowledge to separate right from wrong. Only the wise know to distinguish between holy and profane, between pure and impure.[78] Thus *teshuvah* is identical with *binah*.

The *ba'al teshuvah* becomes aware that sin is a partition between G-d and man. Sin disturbs the balance of the universe, sundering its unity. "He who transgresses the precepts of the *Torah* causes a defect, as it were, above; a defect below; a defect in himself; a defect to all worlds."[79]

The word *teshuvah* can be read as *tashuv-hey* — returning, restoring the *hey*...for when man sins he causes the letter *hey* to be removed from the Divine Name.[80] The Divine Name, the manifestation of G-dliness, is no longer whole. The *hey* has been severed, leaving the other three letters to spell *hoy*, the Biblical exclamation for woe.[81]

"Woe to them that call evil good, and good evil... woe to them that they are wise in their own eyes...."[82]

In turn, "he who does *teshuvah* causes the *hey* to be restored...and the redemption depends on this."[83] *Teshuvah* restores the *hey*, recompletes the Holy Name, reestablishes unity, frees the soul. "*Teshuvah* corrects everything — it rectifies above, rectifies below, rectifies the penitent, rectifies the whole universe."[84]

The *bushah* of *teshuvah* relates only initially to the past. It develops further into an awareness of personal insignificance in the presence of Divine Majesty.[85] On this higher level it signifies *bitul hayesh* (total self-negation). It diverts one's sights from concern with self to concern with the

Ultimate. Thus it ignites a consuming desire to be restored to and absorbed in the Divine Presence: "My soul thirsts for G-d, for the living G-d — when shall I come and be seen in the Presence of G-d...."[86] "Oh G-d, You are my G-d, I seek You earnestly. My soul thirsts for You, my flesh longs for You, in a dry and wary land without water...for Your loving-kindness is better than life...."[87]

This longing of the *ba'al teshuvah* is more intense than that of the *tzaddik*, the saint who never sinned. Having been removed from G-dliness, the *ba'al teshuvah* wants to make up for lost time, for lost opportunities. The energy and passion once expended on nonsense and improprieties are now directed, in ever increasing measure, towards good. He reaches out with all strength, and thus prompted, leaps to levels unattainable by the *tzaddik*.[88]

His former transgressions, now responsible for his efforts and achievements, are thus sublimated. His descent, in effect, generated his ascent. The former sins are thus converted into veritable merits.[89]

The status requiring *teshuvah* is coupled with grief, heart-breaking remorse.[90] The possibility of *teshuvah* generates hope, faith, confidence: "The heart being firm and certain in G-d that He desires to show kindness, and is gracious and compassionate, generously forgiving the instant one pleads for His forgiveness and atonement. Not the faintest vestige of doubt dilutes this absolute conviction."[91]

The act of *teshuvah* results in joy. For every step away from sin is a step closer to virtue. Every move away from the darkness of evil is a move closer to the light of virtue, coming ever closer to G-d. This fact must fill the heart with joy, a true and encompassing joy and happiness, even as the lost child rejoices in having found the way home.[92]

Indeed, this deep sense of joy, filling one's whole being, is the very test and proof of sincere *teshuvah*.[93]

The Universality of Teshuvah

The conventional translation for *teshuvah* is repentance. This, however, is but one aspect, the aspect related to error, to sins of omission or commission. The literal and real translation is "return."

Return implies a two-fold movement. There is a source of origin from which one moved away and to which one wants to return.

The descent of the soul into this world is a move away. Regardless of the lofty purposes to be achieved, the sublime goals to be attained, the fact remains that it is an exile. For the soul in its pristine state is bound up and absorbed in its source, in the very "bond of life with the Eternal." From this Place of Glory, the manifest Presence of G-d, the soul is vested in a physical body, related to matter, exposed to and involved with the very antitheses of spirituality, of holiness.

To retain that original identity, to regain that original bond, that is the ultimate meaning of *teshuvah*. "And the spirit returns unto G-d who gave it."[94]

Teshuvah tata'a, the lower level of *teshuvah*, is rectification, an erasure of the past. On a higher level, *teshuvah* is "coming home," reunion. The child separated and lost, driven to return with a consuming passion, pleads: "It is Your countenance, G-d, that I seek! Do not conceal Your countenance from me!"[95] The innermost point of the heart longs for Divinity so intensely that "his soul is bonded to the love of G-d, continuously enraptured by it like the love-sick whose mind is never free from his passion . . . and as Solomon expressed allegorically:[96] 'For I am sick with love.'"[97]

This higher sense of *teshuvah* — *teshuvah ila'a*, supreme *teshuvah* — relates to the *tzaddik*, the faultless, as well.

The *Torah* is given to all of Israel, to every Jew. Nothing in *Torah* is superfluous. Nothing in *Torah* is the exclusive heritage of some only. Everything in *Torah* speaks to every individual, relates to every one. It is only by way of the whole *Torah* that anyone can become a whole person. Every *mitzvah* serves its purpose. Every instruction is directly relevant to the macrocosm of the universe and the microcosm of every man.

Teshuvah is an integral part of *Torah*. It manifests itself in numerous precepts and instructions. "Every one of the prophets charged the people concerning *teshuvah*."[98] *Teshuvah* thus must relate to the righteous, to the saint, no less than to the sinner. Alternatively, the righteous would be missing out on a significant part of *Torah*. *Teshuvah ila'a* thus relates to the *tzaddik* as well.[99]

Teshuvah ila'a reaches where a normative ascent, a behavior that is faultless yet gradual and normative, cannot reach. It moves man to jump, to leap, blinding him to everything but his objective, disregarding all and any obstacles in the pursuit and attainment of the ultimate goal. In this context the *tzaddik*, too, becomes a *ba'al teshuvah*, "one possessed of *teshuvah*,"[100] a personification of *teshuvah*.

Teshuvah ila'a does not mean a withdrawal of man from the world. It reveals G-d in the world: omnipresence in the most literal sense, an encompassing awareness and a penetrating consciousness of the reality and presence of G-d. "To cleave unto Him, for He is your life,"[101] "there is nothing else beside Him."[102] There is a total negation of ego, a total submersion of personal will in the Supreme Will. Not two entities brought together, but absorption and union to the point of unity.

*   *   *

"This *mitzvah* which I command you this day is not beyond your reach nor is it far off...."[103]

Generally, this verse refers to the entire *Torah*. In context with the preceding passage it is also interpreted to refer specifically to the principle of *teshuvah*:[104] "Even if your outcasts be in the outermost parts of Heaven"[105] and you are under the power of the nations, you can yet return unto G-d and do "according to all that I command you this day."[106] For *teshuvah* "is not beyond reach nor is it far off,"[107] but "it is exceedingly near to you, in your mouth and in your heart to do it."[108]

"One hour of bliss in the World to Come is better than all the life of this world"; yet "one hour of *teshuvah* and good deeds in this world is better than all the life in the World to Come."[109]

> *"Well," said the Rebbe, "do* teshuvah, *and the rest will follow of itself!"*

Anthropomorphism and Metaphors
—————— *Rabbi Dr. J. Immanuel Schochet*

Anthropomorphism

The terminology of *Kabbalah* and *Chassidism*, and thus in the expositions following, is highly anthropomorphic. The terms are borrowed from human concepts and the empirical world. The reason is because these are the only type of words that man can use in any meaningful way. The forms of spatial-temporal concepts are imposed upon the mind of man who lives in a spatial-temporal world.

It is for this very reason that the *Torah*, the Prophets and our Sages use anthropomorphic language, as it is stated: "The *Torah* speaks in the language of man."[1] For:

> "Had they limited themselves to abstract terms and concepts appropriate to G-d, we would have understood neither the terms nor the concepts. The words and ideas used have accordingly to be such as are adapted to the hearer's mental capacity so that the subject would first sink into his mind in the corporeal sense in which the concrete terms are understood. Then we can proceed to an understanding that the presentation is only approximate and metaphorical, and that the reality is too subtle, too exalted and remote for us to comprehend its subtlety.

"The wise thinker will endeavor to strip the husk of the terms (i.e., their materialistic meaning) from the kernel, and will raise his conception step by step until he will at last attain to as much knowledge of the truth as his intellect is capable of apprehending."[2]

Thus it is to be kept in mind at all times that the terms and concepts need to be stripped of all and any temporal, spatial and corporeal connotations. All and any anthropomorphic notions and concepts, strictly speaking, are non-ascribable to the Divinity, as Scripture states explicitly: "To whom then will you liken G-d? Or what likeness will you compare to Him?... To whom will you liken Me that I should be equal, says the Holy One." (*Isaiah* 40:18, 25).

This cardinal premise was adopted by Maimonides as the third in his compilation of the "Thirteen Fundamental Principles of Faith."[3]

At the same time, however, it should also be noted that the anthropomorphic terminology used in Scripture, by the mystics and by others, is not arbitrary just because it is under the protection of the above qualification. Rather, these terms are carefully chosen and possess a profound meaning.

The Rabbinic-Midrashic and mystical writings abound with references to the idea that the world below in general, and man in particular, are created in the "image" of the "world above."[4] All the categories to be found in the world below and in man are homonymous representations of, and allusions to, certain supernal concepts and notions to which they correspond.

To be sure, there is no likeness whatever between G-d and the Creation, and on the supernal levels of the strictly spiritual realm there are no such things as eyes, ears, hands and so on, nor such activities and affections as hearing, seeing, walking, talking and so on. However, all these spatial-temporal activities and concepts do symbolize, and, indeed, for that reason come into being in correspondence to the original supernal, strictly and purely spiritual, categories.

In a widely quoted passage, R. Joseph Gikatilla aptly explains this correspondence-relationship by means of the following analogy. When writing the name of a person on a piece of paper, there is surely no likeness, link or relationship between the written letters or words on paper and the physio-mental entity of the person whose name has been recorded. Even so, that writing is a symbol or sign relating to, calling to mind and denoting the full concrete entity of that person.

Thus it is with the anthropomorphic and anthropopathic concepts and terms. There is no concrete or direct link or likeness between them and the meanings they seek to express, but nonetheless, they are corresponding signs and symbols relating to, and denoting, specific categories, notions and concepts that are of a strictly spiritual nature, non-spatial and non-temporal.[5]

This, then, is the way the anthropomorphic terminology is to be understood.[6]

The Man Metaphor

In discussing Divinity relative to the universe, the favorite metaphor of the mystics (as of many philosophers) is the analogy to man. Theological concepts and the G-d-world relationship are often explained in terms of soul-body relationship and in particular in terms of the various soul-powers, their faculties, functions and manifestations.

The "proof-texts" for this usage are the verse "From my flesh I envisage G-d" (*Job* 19:26) and the Rabbinic analogy, "Just as the soul permeates the whole body... sees but is not seen... sustains the whole body... is pure... abides in the innermost precincts... is unique in the body... does not eat and does not drink... no man knows where its place is... so the Holy One, blessed is He...."[7] This, too, in a sense, follows on the above-mentioned principle of a "terrestrial-supernal correspondence."[8]

But even while an understanding of the soul is helpful in understanding matters relating to the Divinity, this is but an anthropomorphic approximation which cannot be carried too far and needs to be qualified. It must be remembered, as R. Schneur Zalman points out, that in some respects the analogy breaks down, and is completely inadequate:

"This parallel is only to appease the ear. In truth, however, the analogy has no similarity whatever to the object of comparison. For the human soul... is affected by the accidents of the body and its pain... while the Holy One, blessed is He, is not, Heaven forbid, affected by the accidents of the world and its changes, nor by the world itself; they do not effect any change in Him...."[9]

Also, "The soul and the body are actually distinct, one from the other, in their very sources, for the source of the body and its essence does not come into being from the soul...."[10] Thus while the body may be fully subordinate to the soul, they are, nevertheless, two distinct entities. In contrast, "in relation to the Holy One, blessed is He, who brings everything into existence *ex nihilo*, everything is absolutely nullified, just as the light of the sun is nullified in the sun itself."[11]

The Light Metaphor

Just as the soul provides a favorite metaphor, so we find that the term "light" is favored by the mystics to describe the various emanations and manifestations of the Divinity.[12] This term is carefully chosen for a number of reasons. R. Joseph Albo sees in it the following advantages that may analogously be related to G-d:

(i) The existence of light cannot be denied.

(ii) Light is not a corporeal thing.

(iii) Light causes the faculty of sight and the visible colors to pass from potentiality to actuality.

(iv) Light delights the soul.

(v) One who has never seen a luminous body in his life cannot conceive colors nor the agreeableness and delightfulness of light.

(vi) And even he who has seen luminous objects cannot endure to gaze upon an intense light, and if he insists upon gazing beyond his power of endurance, his eyes become dim so that he cannot see thereafter even that which is normally visible.

By possessing all these qualities, light bears a greater similarity to the things which are free from matter than anything else to which such things may be compared, and hence they are compared to light so as to make the matter intelligible.[13]

Likewise, R. Joseph Ergas lists the following advantages:[14] (a) Light is the most subtle and tenuous of all sense-perceptions.[15] (b) Light has numerous qualities characteristic of the Divine emanations, as, for example:

(i) Light is emitted from the luminary without ever becoming separated from it. Even when its source is concealed or removed, thus no longer emitting perceptible light, the previous rays do not remain entities separate from the luminary but are withdrawn with it. This is a unique quality of light which is not shared with any other substance.

(ii) Light spreads itself instantaneously.

(iii) Light irradiates all physical objects and is able to penetrate unhindered all transparent objects.

(iv) Light does not mix and mingle with another substance.

(v) Light *per se* never changes. The perception of more or less intense light, or of differently colored lights, is not due to any change in the light *per se* but is due to external factors.

(vi) Light is essential to life in general.

(vii) Light is received and absorbed relative to the capacities of the recipient; and so on.[16]

But here again, this term is only an homonymous approximation used by way of metaphor and analogy. It is not to be taken in its full, literal sense. R. Joseph Albo already cautions that "No error should be made to the effect that intellectual light is something emanating from a corporeal object like sensible light."[17] R. Moses Cordovero is still more emphatic in warning that this metaphor must not be carried too far; "For there is no image whatever that can be imagined that is not corporeal."[18]

Indeed, R. Menachem Mendel of Lubavitch shows how, in some respects, this analogy, too, evidently breaks down and is inadequate. For example, the emittance of perceptible light from its source is automatic and intrinsically necessary: the luminary cannot withhold the light. Therefore, this restrictive quality cannot be ascribed to the emanations of the Omnipotent.[19]

In conclusion, then, as the mystics never tire to say, it cannot be mentioned too often or stressed too much that all terms and concepts related to the Divinity must be stripped of all and any temporal, spatial and corporeal connotations and must be understood in a strictly spiritual sense.

Reprinted from *Mystical Concepts in Chassidism*, by J. Immanuel Schochet, published by Kehot Publication Society, New York, U.S.A.

Sources and Notes

The Dynamics of Teshuvah

1. *Proverbs* 3:18.
2. *Zohar* III:53b.
3. *Zohar* III:260a. See *Likkutei Sichot* (English), vol. I, p. XV.
4. *Deuteronomy* 30:11-14.
5. *Midrash Rabbah, Genesis* 8:2; *Talmud, Pessachim* 54a.
6. *Midrash Rabbah, Genesis* 1:2.
7. *Zohar* II:161a; *Midrash Rabbah, Genesis* 1:1.
8. *See Likkutei Sichot* (English), volume I, Bereishit section III.
9. See *Mystical Concepts in Chassidism*, chapter I, section 1, and notes 4 and 5 *a.l.*; *Likkutei Sichot* (English), volume I, p. 199 and note b,*a.l.* cf. *Zohar* I:134b and III:202a.
10. *Talmud, Macot* 23b; *Zohar* I:170b.
11. See *Tanya*, chapters 23 and 37; *Igeret Hateshuvah*, chapter 1.
12. See *Tanya*, chapters 24 and 37; *Igeret Hateshuvah*, chapter 1.
13. *Talmud, Yoma* 36b.
14. *Isaiah* 59:2. See *Igeret Hateshuvah*, chapter 5.
15. *Deuteronomy* 30:6 and 30:20. See *Igeret Hateshuvah, chapter 9; and Igeret Hakodesh*, section 4.
16. See above notes 11-12.
17. *Talmud Yerushalmi, Shabbat* 14:3.
18. *Zohar* III:13b and 16a.
19. *Talmud, Sotah* 3a. See *Tanya*, chapters 19 and 24. cf. R. Sholom Ber Schneerson of Lubavitch, *Kuntres Uma'ayon* I:1, IV, and XVI:2.
20. See *Akeidat Yitzchak*, Sha'ar 73. cf. *Kuntres Uma'ayon* XIII:1, XIV and XVI:2; Rabbi J.I. Schneersohn, *Torat Hachassidut*, XX-XXIV; *Likkutei Sichot*, volume I, Bo, section IX.
21. See Maimonides, *Hilchot Yesodei Hatorah*, chapter 4.
22. See *Tanya*, chapters 37-38.
23. See *Tanya*, chapters 8-9. Cf. *Mystical Concepts in Chassidism*, chapters X-XI.
24. See Maimonides, *Hilchot Teshuvah*, chapter 5. Cf. *Mystical Concepts in Chassidism*, chapter XI.

25. *Zohar* III:187a.
26. See *Tanya*, chapters 35 and 53.
27. See R. Chaim Vital, *Sha'arei Kedushah* III:2.
28. *Genesis* 4:7. See *Talmud, Yoma* 19b f., and Rashi *a.l.*; and cf. *Talmud, Succah* 52b.
29. *Ecclesiastes* 7:20.
30. Rashi on *Genesis* 1:1; *Zohar Chadash*, Noach, 21d; *Midrash Rabbah*, *Genesis* 12:15.
31. *Exodus* 34:6.
32. *Psalms* 130:1.
33. *Zohar* III:69b. See also *Pirkei de R. Eliezer*, chapter 3.
34. *Jeremiah* 33:25.
35. *Talmud, Pessachim* 68b.
36. See *Akeidat Yitzchak*, sha'ar 63.
37. See *Mystical Concepts in Chassidism*, chapter III, section 5, *s.v.* Tiferet, and especially note 103.
38. *Genesis* 8:21. See also *ibid.* 6:5.
39. See also *Ezekiel* chapter 33, and *Zohar Chadash*, Noach, 22a-b.
40. *Moreh Nevuchim* III:36.
41. *Zohar* II:106a; *Zohar Chadash*, Bereshit, 20d; *Talmud Yerushalmi*, *Peah* I:1. See *Tanya*, chapter 25, and *Igeret Hateshuvah*, chapter 4.
42. See *Talmud, Berachot* 34b; *Hilchot Teshuvah* 7:5.
43. See *Likkutei Sichot*, vol. IV, p. 1144f.
44. See *Igeret Hateshuvah*, chapter 4. Cf. *Reishit Chochmah*, Sha'ar Hakedushah, chapter 17, and note there the original interpretation of the Elisha ben Abuya affair in *Talmud, Chagigah* 15a.
45. See *Hilchot Teshuvah* 2:4.
46. *Talmud, Berachot* 34b; *Hilchot Teshuvah* 7:4. See also *Akeidat Yitzchak*, sha'ar 100.
47. See *Talmud, Shabbat* 105b; *Talmud, Succah* 52a-b.
48. *Zohar* I:129a-b. Cf. *Talmud, Avodah Zara* 17a: Rebbi wept and said: Some acquire eternal life after many years, others in one hour!
49. *Talmud, Kiddushin* 49b; *Shulchan Aruch*, Even Ha'ezer, 38:31. The principle that a *ba'al teshuvah* is superior to a *tzaddik* (above note 46) appears to be disputed in the *Talmud* without any explicit resolution. By what authority, then, did many adopt this view as a ruling? Many texts deal with this issue; *cf.* the glossary notes of the Rebbe שליט״א on *Sefer Hamaamarim 5709*, p. 183f., and the references cited there. The famed Gaon of Rogatchov, R. Joseph Rosen, refers with ingenious insight to the law just cited: *per force* we must say that a *ba'al teshuvah* is either equal or superior to the *tzaddik*, or else the condition could never be fulfilled! See S.J. Zevin, *Hamo'adim Behalachah*, p. 67f.
50. See *Hilchot Teshuvah* 2:2-3; *Igeret Hateshuvah*, chapter 1. See also *Tanya*, chapter 29, and *Igeret Hakodesh*, section 10.
51. See above the quote corresponding to note 33. Also *Talmud, Pessachim*

54a, and *Midrash Rabbah, Genesis* 1:5. "The greatness of *teshuvah* lies in its preceding the creation of the world"; *Midrash Tehillim* 90:12.

52. See R. Dov Ber of Mezeritch, *Or Torah*, sections 245, 391 and 444.

53. *Zohar* I:266b; and III:247b.

54. *Keter Shem Tov*, section 56; *Tzavaat Harivash*, section 69, and the notes *a.l.*

55. See *Igeret Hateshuvah*, chapters 1-3.

56. See *Sefer Chassidim* (Parma), section 37; *Rake'ach Hagadol*, Teshuvah.

57. *Hilchot Teshuvah* 6:2.

58. Maimonides, *Hilchot Mikvaot*, 11:12. Note the analogy between *teshuvah* and the purifying waters of a *mikvah*. The *Midrash* goes a step further: *Teshuvah* is more than a *mikvah;* it is like the sea, immersion in which also effects purification. A *mikvah* is subject to limitations of time and space. It is limited to a distinct location (a building), and is not always accessible or available. The sea, however, transcends these limitations: it is always accessible and available, if not in one particular spot then in another. "*Teshuvah* is like the sea, which is never barred so that whoever desires to bathe in it can do so whenever he desires." *Midrash Tehillim* 65:4; *Pessikta de R. Kahana*, section 25; and see the marginal references there.

59. *Psalms* 36:4-5.

60. *Talmud, Berachot* 7a.

61. Here, indeed, is the ultimate test for the sincere and true *teshuvah:* though again exposed to the same temptations, the *ba'al teshuvah* is now in control of himself and will not succumb. Thus the symptoms disappear. See *Talmud, Yoma* 86b.

62. *Talmud, Berachot* 10a.

63. *Talmud, Yoma* 86a. Cf. *Tikunei Zohar* 22:66b.

64. *Talmud, Avot* 4:11.

65. *Talmud, Sotah* 3b.

66. *Talmud, Succah* 52b.

67. Cf. *Tzavaat Harivash*, section 116, and the notes *a.l.*

68. Tzemach Tzedek, *Derech Mitzvotecha*, Mitzvat Viduy Teshuvah, chapter 1. See also *Igeret Hateshuvah*, chapter 7.

69. *Joel* 2:13.

70. *Talmud, Yerushalmi, Ta'anit* 2:1.

71. *Zohar* I:79b; III:122a and 216a. *Igeret Hateshuvah*, chapter 9.

72. Liturgy, Morning Prayers. For the significance of this phrase see *Reishit Chochmah*, Sha'ar Ha'ahavah chapter 5; and also *Tanya*, part II *(Sha'ar Hayichud)*, chapters 1-3.

73. *Jeremiah* 2:13. Cf. *Igeret Hateshuvah*, chapter 7.

74. See *Sefer Halikutim - Tzemach Tzedek*, s.v. *Teshuvah*, p. 352f.

75. *Talmud, Berachot* 12b; *Netivot Olam*, Teshuvah, ch. 5. "Shamefacedness leads to fear of sin; hence it was said that it is a good sign if a man is

shamefaced. No man who experiences shame will easily sin..."; *Talmud, Nedarim* 20a; cf. *Talmud, Yevamot* 79a.

76. *Isaiah* 6:10.
77. *Talmud, Megillah* 17b.
78. See *Talmud, Yerushalmi, Berachot* 5:2; and Rashi on *Talmud, Berachot* 33a.
79. *Zohar* III:122a.
80. *Ibid.* See *Igeret Hateshuvah*, chapter 4. The word *teshuvah* is divisible into these two components: *tashuv-hei*. Note that the letter *hey* represents the physical world: This world was created with the *hey*... because it is like an *exedra* (closed on three sides and open on the fourth), and whosoever wishes to go astray may do so (has the choice to let himself fall through the open bottom of the *hey*.) And why is the "leg" of the *hey* suspended (leaving an opening at the side, from above)? To indicate that whosoever repents is permitted to reenter. *Talmud, Menachot* 29b, see there.
81. *Zohar* III:74b, see there.
82. *Isaiah* 5:20. Note the frequent repetition of this exclamation in that chapter, as elsewhere in the Bible, with reference to sinners.
83. *Zohar* III:122a; *Igeret Hateshuvah*, chapter 4.
84. *Zohar* III:122a.
85. This is the concept of *Yirat Boshet*, the penetrating awe before the Majesty of G-d to the point of truly sensing personal insignificance. See *Hilchot Yesodei Hatorah* 2:2 and 4:12; *Tanya*, chapter 3; *Igeret Hakodesh*, end of section 15. See also R. Shmuel of Lubavitch, *Mayim Rabim 5636*, chapter 136.
86. *Psalms* 42:3. See *Hilchot Yesodei Hatorah* 2:2.
87. *Psalms* 63:2ff.
88. *Zohar* I:129b; *Tanya*, chapter 7; *Igeret Heteshuvah*, chapter 8; *Igeret Hakodesh*, section 10. Cf. also *Zohar* III:16b and 195a, and *Zohar Chadash*, Balak, 54b, for the reason why the *ba'al teshuvah* surpasses the *tzaddik*.
89. *Talmud, Yoma* 86b. See *Tanya*, chapter 7.
90. See *Igeret Hateshuvah*, chapter 7.
91. *Igeret Hateshuvah*, chapter 11.
92. See R. Dov Ber of Lubavitch, *Derech Chayim*, chapter 1. Cf. *Igeret Hateshuvah*, chapters 10-11, and *Torat Hachassidut*, XXVIII.
93. R. Dov Ber of Lubavitch, *Poke'ach Ivrim*, section 15. Cf. *Zohar* III: 15b-16a.
94. *Ecclesiastes* 12:7.
95. *Psalms* 27:8-9. See *Igeret Hakodesh*, section 4.
96. *Song* 2:5.
97. *Hilchot Teshuvah* 10:3.
98. *Ibid.* 7:5. Cf. *Talmud, Berachot* 34b.
99. See *Torah Or*, Vayechi, 45a-b; *Likkutei Torah*, Shabbat Shuvah, 66c-d; *Mayim Rabim 5636*, chapter 135.

100. See *Zohar* II:106b.
101. *Deuteronomy* 30:20; see above note 15.
102. *Deuteronomy* 4:35. See *Tanya*, part II (Sha'ar Hayichud), chapter 6.
103. *Deuteronomy* 30:11.
104. Commentary of Nachmanides, a.l. See also *Ikkarim* IV:25; and *Akeidat Yitzchak*, sha'ar 100.
105. *Deuteronomy* 30:4.
106. *Ibid.* 2.
107. *Ibid.* 11.
108. *Ibid.* 14.
109.   *Talmud, Avot* 4:17. See *Tanya*, chapter 4; and *Igeret Hakodesh*, section 1. Note that the term *sha'ah achat* (one hour) can also be interpreted as "one turn" (see *Genesis* 4:4-5, and Rashi *a.l.*); cf. the Maggid's *Or Torah, Hossafot*, section 38; *Likkutei Torah, Rosh Hashanah*, 61a. Our text, then, may also be read as "one *turn* of *teshuvah* and good deeds..."; see *Torat Hachassidut*, XXIV.

Anthropomorphism and Metaphors

1. *Talmud, Berachot* 31b; *Mechilta*, and *Tanchuma* on *Exodus* 15:7 and 19:18; *Sifra* on *Leviticus* 20:2.
2. R. Bachya ibn Pakuda, *Chovot Halevovot, Sha'ar Hayichud*: chapter 10. Cf. *Otzar Hageonim, Berachot*, Responsa no. 357 (I:p. 131), and Comment, no. 271 (II:p. 92); R. Judah Halevi, *Kuzary* IV:5; Maimonides, *Hilchot Yesodei Hatorah* I:7-12, and *Moreh Nevuchim* I:26, 33, 35f. and 46; *Tanya* II:10.
3. *Commentary on Mishnah, Sanhedrin*, Introduction to chapter 10. Cf. *Hilchot Teshuvah* III:7; *Moreh Nevuchim* I:36 (and the references to Maimonides, *supra*, note 2).
4. *Midrash Tanchuma*, Pekudei:3; *Avot de R. Nathan*, ch. 31; *Midrash Rabbah, Ecclesiastes* I:4; *Zohar* I:38a, 140a, 205b; *ibid.* II:20a, 48b, 75bf.; *ibid.* III:65b, 117a; *et passim*. See also *Chovot Halevovot*, I: chapter 10, and II: chapters 2, 3 and 5. (Most of these sources are quoted in the discussion of the "correspondence-theory" in J.I. Schochet, *"The Psychological System of R. Schneur Zalman of Liadi,"* parts I and II, *Di Yiddishe Heim*, volume XI (New York 1970), nos. 3-4.)
5. *Sha'arei Orah*, Sha'ar I (ed. Warsaw 1883, p. 2b). Cf. R. Solomon ibn Aderet, *Chidushei Harashba al Agadot Hashass*, on *Talmud, Bava Batra 74b* (Jerusalem 1966, p. 90). For a fuller discussion of the mystics' view of anthropomorphisms see R. Meir ibn Gabbai, *Avodat Hakodesh*, part III, especially chapter 26ff. and chapter 65; R. Moses

Cordovero, *Pardes Rimonim*, section XXII *(Sha'ar Hakinuyim)*, especially chapter 2; R. Isaiah Horowitz, *Shenei Luchot Habrit*, *Toldot
Adam: Bayit Neeman*; (all of which quote R. Joseph Gikatilla). In
addition, the whole of R. Moses Cordovero's *Shi'ur Komah* is devoted
to this topic. See also R. Joseph Ergas, *Shomer Emunim* I:24*f*.

R. Isaiah Horowitz *(ad loc. cit.*, p. 10d) makes the interesting point
that strictly speaking it is not that "the *Torah* speaks in the language of
man," but — in accordance with the aforesaid — exactly the other way
around, because all terrestrial concepts are allusions to supernal ones!
Cf. *Peri Etz Chayim*, Sha'ar Hakorbanot, chapter 6, *s.v.* Baraita de R.
Yishmael; *Likkutei Sichot*, volume II, p. 363*f*.

6. This should be remembered with particular regard to the so-called
"erotic" concepts and symbolisms, like the frequent occurrence of
terms as "masculine" and "feminine" and "conjunctio" and so on.

In general these denote the aspects of the active, emanating
(influencing) category and the passive, receiving qualities and categories, the mode or form of emanation-reception and so forth (see *Igeret
Hakodesh*, section XV, note 9). "The whole universe functions according to the principium of masculine and feminine" (R. Chayim Vital,
Etz Chaim 11:6). "There are four principles: masculine and feminine
(זו״ן); Judgment *(Din)* and compassion *(Rachamim)*; upper and lower;
influencer or emanator *(Mashpiah)* and influenced *(Mushpa*; also
called *Mekabel* — recipient). As a rule, the masculine corresponds to
compassion, upper and emanated; and the female corresponds to
judgment, lower and recipient;" *idem., Peri Etz Chaim*, Hakdamah II:
end of Derush 2 (ed. Tel Aviv 1966, p. 13a), and *Olat Tamid*,
beginning of Sha'ar Hatefillah *(ed.* Tel Aviv 1963, p. 2a).

Actually, such terminology is not uniquely *Kabbalistic*. It may be
found in the *Talmudic* writings — [*Talmud, Bava Batra* 74b: "All that
the Holy One, blessed is He, created in His world, He created male and
female"; see the commentaries *ad loc.*, and especially *Chidushei
Harashba al Agadot Hashass, op. cit.*, pp. 91*ff.*, quoted at length by R.
Jacob ibn Chabib in his *Hakotev* on *Ayin Ya'akov*] as well as in the
philosophical literature [*e.g., Moreh Nevuchim*, Introduction, and
ibid., I: chapters 6 and 17, and III: chapters 8 and 12].

R. Schneur Zalman explains at length why the mystics purposely
chose such delicate and seemingly peculiar terminology; see *Likkutei
Torah* V:9a, and *Biurei Hazohar*, ed. R. Dov Ber of Lubavitch (New
York 1955), Noach: pp. 6a*ff*. The earlier mystics, too, elaborate on the
usage of these particular concepts; see *Pardess Rimonim* XXII:1; *Shi'ur
Komah*, chapter 18; *Shenei Luchot Habrit, ad loc. cit.* (p. 8d*f*.); *Shomer
Emunim* I:26*f*.

7. *Talmud, Berachot* 10a; *Midrash Tehillim (ed.* Buber) 103:4, 5 (see
notes *ad loc.*); *Tikunei Zohar* 13:28a. See *Shomer Emunim* II:9; *Igeret
Hakodesh*, beginning of section XV, and section XXV and XXIX.

8. See references *supra*, note 4.
9. *Tanya*, I, chapter 42.
10. *Ibid.*, II:6.
11. *Ibid.* See at length R. Menachem Mendel of Lubavitch, *Sefer Hacha-kirah* I:8 (New York 1955, pp. 7b-8b and 26a-b). Cf. *infra*, chapter 2, note 18, and chapter 3, end of section 4.
12. This metaphor, too, like the previous one, abounds in the *Talmudic Midrashic* and medieval-philosophic writings; see, *e.g.*, *Talmud*, *Berachot* 17a, 64a and so forth (the concept of *Ziv Hashechinah*; the radiation of the *Shechinah*); *Sifre*, and *Midrashim*, on *Numbers* 6:25; *Pirkei de R. Eliezer*, ch. 3; *Midrash Rabbah*, *Leviticus*, chapter 31 (especially paragraph 6); *Midrash Rabbah*, *Numbers*, 15:5; etc. See further R. Sa'adiah Gaon, *Emunot Vede'ot* III:10; *Kuzary* II:7-8 and III:17, and especially IV:3; *Moreh Nevuchim* I; ends of chapters 5, 19 and 25, and *ibid.*, chapter 76; also, R. Moses Narboni, *Commentary on Moreh Nevuchim* I:35; and so on. In general, though, the philosophical works use mostly the term *shefa'* (effluence; emanation) rather than *or*; see more on that in R. Menachem Mendel of Lubavitch, *Derech Mitzvotecha*, *Haamanat Elokut*: chapter 5 (New York 1956, p. 50b *f.*).

   The mystics have a special affinity for the term *Or* because its numerical value (*gimatriya*) is equivalent to that of *raz* (mystery): "'Let there be light' (*Gen.* 1:3) — i.e., let there be *Raz* (Mystery; Concealment); for *Raz* and *Or* are one thing"; *Zohar* I: 140a and *Zohar Chadash*, Bereishit: 8d; see *Tikunei Zohar* 21:53b, and cf. R. Moses Cordovero, *Or Ne'erav* (Fuerth, 1701), III: chapter 4.
13. *Ikkarim* II:29.
14. *Shomer Emunim* II:11.
15. Cf. *Kuzary* IV:3: "The noblest and finest of all material things...."
16. Cf. *Tanya* I, chapter 52, and *ibid.*, II:10. See also R. Schneur Zalman, *Torah Or*, *Vayakhel*: 87a-b, and *Siddur 'im Perush Hamilot*, pp. 48a *ff.* and 164c *ff.*

   Obviously this "descriptive analysis" of light is based on the general human perception — the sense-perception — of it, while an exact "scientific analysis" is not really relevant to our purposes. Apart from the fact that this metaphor is qualified in any case (as we shall see), they are the *empirical perceptions* that make the use of this analogy so attractive and helpful in our context.
17. *Ikkarim*, *ad loc. cit.*; see there at length.
18. R. Moses Cordovero, *Elima Rabbaty*, I:i:9 (p. 4b). See also *Emunot Vede'ot* I:3 and II:2 with regard to light being an accident (as opposed to substance) and having a limit and boundary.
19. *Derech Mitzvotecha*, *ad loc. cit.* (*supra*, note 12). See also *Shi'ur Komah*, chapters 3-4.

Glossary

Those Hebrew words and expressions that are translated or explained within the text have, in the main, been omitted from the Glossary.

Acharonim. lit. Later ones. Jewish Codifiers and commentators from about the sixteenth century to the present day.

Aggadah. lit. Narration. Whereas the *Halachah* deals with Jewish law and ordinances, all other matters such as prayers, philosophy, theology, ethics, history, etc. are classified as *Aggadah*.

Alef Bet. The first and second letters of the Hebrew alphabet. Expression used to refer to the Hebrew alphabet.

Amoraim. lit. Speakers or interpreters. The term was applied to all teachers in Palestine and Babylonia who flourished during a period of about 300 years from the death of Judah I (219 CE) to the redaction of the Babylonian Talmud (about 500 CE). The activity of the *Amoraim* consisted primarily in interpreting the *Mishnah*, although they did offer legal opinions of their own.

ARI. See Luria, Isaac.

Asiyah. Fourth of the "Four Worlds" generally translated as "action." But this term is neither definitive nor descriptive, since all "Four Worlds" are in a sense "action." *Asiyah* should be understood as the final stage in the creative process. For example, in desiring to build a house, the following four stages would be involved from the conception of the idea until its materialization:
(a) A general idea, as yet undefined.
(b) A definite idea of the house in mind.

(c) Architectural plan, or design.

(d) Actual building of the house.

These four stages would generally correspond to the "Four Worlds."

Atzilut. World of Emanation; highest of the "Four Worlds." In *Chabad*, etymologically connected with *etzel* (near), i.e. nearest to the Source of Creation, the *Ein Sof*, hence still in a state of Infinity. See *Asiyah*.

Baal Shem Tov. lit. Master of the Good Name. Applied to Rabbi Israel Baal Shem Tov, founder of *Chassidism*.

Ba'al teshuvah (pl. ba'alei teshuvah). A penitent. See *teshuvah*.

Baraita (pl. **Baraitot**). Aramaic word for "outside." A *baraita* is an "outside" *mishnah*. This term includes every *halachah*, *halachic midrash* and historical or *aggadic* tradition which is "outside" (i.e. not included in) R. Yehuda haNassi's *Mishnah;* some directly connected with a *mishnah* and others independent of the *Mishnah*. The expression *Baraita* is employed in the Babylonian Talmud (it

occurs only once in the Talmud Yerushalmi) mainly to emphasize a view opposed to that of the *Mishnah*.

Benoni. Intermediate category. Those, whose moral character is between *tzaddik* and *rasha*. Not in the *halachic* definition, which is one whose good and bad acts balance the other, but one who never actually commits a wrong, yet evil still inheres in his nature. To be a *benoni* is within the reach of every Jew.

Beriah. World of "Creation," second of the "Four Worlds." A definite state, radically different from *Atzilut*. See *Asiyah*.

BeShT. Popular name by which Rabbi Israel Baal Shem Tov is known. An acronym of *Baal Shem Tov*.

Bet Din. lit. House of Law. Rabbinical Court.

Bet Hamidrash. lit. House of Study. Place of prayer and learning.

Bet Hamikdosh. The Holy Temple in ancient Jerusalem. The first one was built by King Solomon and destroyed by Nebuchadnezzar of Babylon (586 B.C.E.). The second was built by the returning exiles from Babylon and destroyed by Titus of Rome (70 C.E.).

Binah. Understanding; comprehension; intellectual grasp. One of the three primary intellect powers. See also *Chabad*.

Bitul. Nullify; humble.

Chabad. Acronym of *Chochmah* (wisdom), *Binah* (understanding), *Daat* (knowledge). Branch of *chassidic* movement, founded by Rabbi Schneur Zalman, based on intellectual approach to the service of G-d.

Chabadnick(s). Follower(s) of the philosophy of *Chabad*.

Chagat. Acronym of *Chesed, Gevurah, Tiferet*. The primary emotion powers.

Challah (pl. **challot**). Popularly refers to the traditional *Shabbat* and *Yom Tov* loaves of bread. *Challah* was the portion of dough donated to the Priest in Temple times (Numbers 15: 17-21). In post-Temple times the Rabbis ordained that the *challah*, which had to be at least the size of an olive, must be separated and burnt.

Chassid (pl. **chassidim**). Adherent(s) of the *Chassidic* movement; follower(s) of a *Chassidic Rebbe*.

Chassidic. Appertaining to *Chassidism* and *Chassidut*.

Chassidism. Movement founded by Rabbi Israel Baal Shem Tov.

Chassidut. Philosophy of *Chassidism*.

Chesed. Kindness; one of the emotion attributes. See also *Chagat*.

Chochmah. Wisdom; concept. One of the three primary intellect powers. See also *Chabad*.

Daat. Knowledge; concentration; depth. One of the three primary intellect powers. See also *Chabad*.

Ein Sof. The "Endless," "Infinite." Term frequently used in the *Zohar* and later *Kabbalistic* works when referring to G-d.

Elul. Last month of Hebrew calendar. Period of repentance in preparation for *Rosh Hashanah*.

Erev. The day before.

Galut. Exile; diaspora.

Gemarrah. The work based on, and directly interpreting, the *Mishnah*. Together they constitute the *Talmud*.

Gevurah. Might; severity; restraint; one of the emotion attributes. See also *Chagat*.

Halachah. Jewish law.

Halachic. Appertaining to *Halachah*.

Halachist(s). Codifier(s) and/or expounder(s) of Jewish law.

Hashem. lit. the Name; alternative name for G-d.

Havdalah. Prayer marking the end of the Shabbat and/or a Festival.

Hey. Fifth letter of the Hebrew alphabet. Its numerical value is five. As an abbreviation it stands for *Hashem*.

Kabbalah. lit. Received tradition. Esoteric Jewish lore; mysticism; inner interpretation of the *Torah*.

Kabbalat Shabbat. lit. Acceptance of the *Shabbat*. Prayers said to usher in the Shabbat.

Kabbalistic. Appertaining to *Kabbalah*.

Kadosh. Holy.

Kadosh, kadosh, kadosh. lit. holy, holy, holy. The first three words of the phrase "Holy, holy, holy is the L-rd of hosts; the whole earth is full of His glory" (Isaiah 6:3) which appears in a number of places in the liturgy. The three-fold repetition indicates the superlative degree of holiness. "Holy in the highest heaven, holy upon the earth, holy for ever and ever."

Kashrut. *Torah* dietary observances.

Kelipah. Bark or shell. The symbol frequently used in *Kabbalah* to denote evil and the source of sensuous desires in human nature.

Kelipat nogah. Translucent shell. Contains some good, and distinguished from the three completely "dark" *kelipot* containing no good at all. The "animal soul" *(nefesh habahamit)* in the Jew is derived from *kelipat nogah*, by contrast to his "divine soul" *(nefesh elokit)* which is "part" of G-dliness.

Kiddush. Prayer of sanctification

recited on the Shabbat and on Festivals, usually over a cup of wine.

Kipah. Skull cap.

Kos. A goblet. Used for containing wine for *kiddush, havdalah* and other ceremonial occasions.

Lecha Dodi. lit. "Come my beloved..." The opening words of one of the best-known hymns sung in the Friday *Kabbalat Shabbat* service. Written by Solomon (Shlomoh Ha-Levi) Alkabetz in the middle of the sixteenth century. The initial letters of the first eight verses spell out the name of the author. Each verse of this hymn is followed by the refrain: "Come my beloved to meet the bride (Shabbat); let us welcome the presence of the Shabbat." It is customary for the congregation to turn towards the entrance of the synagogue while reciting the last verse.

L'havdil. To distinguish or to separate.

Lubavitch. "Town of love" in the county of Mohilev, White Russia. It became the residence of the heads of the Lubavitch-Chabad movement in 1814 when Rabbi Dovber, son and successor of Rabbi Schneur Zalman settled there. For over a century (until 1916) and, for four generations of *Chabad* leaders, it remained the center of the movement. Hence, the leaders of *Chabad* became known as the "Lubavitcher Rebbes" and their *chassidim* as "Lubavitcher *chassidim.*"

Lulav. Palm branch. One of the four species of plants used on *Succot.*

Luria, Isaac (1534-1572). Born in Jerusalem to German immigrant parents, his surname was Ashkenazi. After being orphaned in early childhood he went to Egypt where he was brought up and educated by his uncle. He lived there as a hermit for thirteen years engrossed in the study of the *Zohar*. In 1569 he went to Tzefat, then the center of *Kabbalistic* study, where he settled. His pupils named him the *Ari* (Lion) *Ha-Kadosh*, an acronym of "Ashkenazi Rabbi Isaac" with the attribute of "the holy." His ideas and teachings, received by his pupils orally, were posthumously recorded by his pupil Rabbi Chaim Vital.

Maariv. Evening prayer.

Machshavah. Thought. The first of the three external "garments" (thought, speech and deed) of the Divine soul.

Maimonides. Rabbi Moshe ben Maimon (Moses Maimonides) (1135-1204), popularly known as the *Rambam*. Greatest Jewish philosopher and codifier of the Middle Ages and distinguished physician. Among his numerous writings, his two greatest literary works are his Code Mishneh Torah (Repetition of the Law) and his philosophical work Moreh Nevuchim (Guide for the Perplexed). These two works have left an indelible mark on Jewish life and scholarship. As a tribute to his greatness it was said of him that: "From Moses unto Moses there arose none like Moses."

Malach (pl. **malachim**). Angel(s).

Matzah. Unleavened bread, eaten on Passover, in place of leavened bread.

Mechilta. Commentary by the Sages on the Book of Exodus.

Meiri. Menachem ben Solomon Perpignan (c.1249-1306). French *talmudist*.

Menorah. Hebrew name for the golden seven-branched candlestick in the sanctuary of the Tabernacle, and in the *Bet Hamikdosh* of old.

Mezuzah. The sacred scroll, containing portions of the *Shema*, affixed on the doorposts of a Jewish home.

Midot. lit. "attributes"; seven in number corresponding to the Seven Days of Creation. Together with the three intellectual powers *Chochmah, Binah* and *Daat* they comprise the ten supernal *sefirot*.

Midrash. Rabbinical homiletical literature, exegesis.

Minhag. Custom.

Mishnah. The codification, by Rabbi Yehuda haNassi, of the Oral Law.

Mishnaic. Appertaining to the *Mishnah*.

Mitzvah (pl. **mitzvot**). Commandment(s); religious obligation(s).

Moshe Rabbenu. Moses, our teacher.

Neshamah. Soul. Usually refers to the Divine soul.

Nigleh. The exoteric (revealed)

part of the *Torah*, as opposed to *nistar*, the esoteric part.

Nistar (pl. **nistarim**). Hidden one(s). Mystic(s). Esoteric.

Olam chesed yiboneh. "The world is built on kindness." (Psalms 89:3).

Pardes. lit. orchard. Acronym of P*eshat*, R*emez*, D*rush* and S*od* (simple meaning, allusions, homiletical interpretations and secrets of the *Torah*). Together they comprise the full depth of the teachings of the *Torah*.

Pnimiyut haTorah. Inner meaning of the *Torah*.

Rasha. Wicked person.

Rebbe. Rabbi and teacher. Leader of a *chassidic* group.

RIF. Name by which Isaac Alfasi (1013-1103) was known. *Talmudic* scholar and commentator.

Rosh Hashanah. lit. Head of the year. First and second days of *Tishrei*. *Rosh Hashanah* is the two-day festival at the beginning of the Jewish New Year.

Savrei Maranan. lit. "Attention gentlemen!" Preface to the blessing on wine at *kiddush*.

Sechel. Intellect. Comprising *Chochmah*, *Binah*, *Daat* (ChaBaD). The first three of the Ten *Sefirot*; sometimes referred to also as *mochin* (brains); also as *immot* (mothers), being the source of the *midot*.

Sefer Torah (pl. **Sifrei Torah**). Scroll(s) of the Law.

Sefirah (pl. **Sefirot**). Divine "attribute(s)," "emanation(s)," or "manifestation(s)," numbering ten, often referred to as the Ten Supernal *Sefirot*. They are divided into two categories: *sechel* (intellect) and *midot* (attributes emotions).

Shabbat (pl. **Shabbatot**). Sabbath(s); The Seventh Day.

Shechinah. Divine Presence.

Shema. Hear. First word of passage of the *Chumash* (Pentateuch) recited daily, in the morning and evening. (Deuteronomy 6:4-9).

Shofar. Ram's horn. Sounded during the month of *Elul*, on *Rosh Hashanah* and at the close of *Yom Kippur*.

Shulchan Aruch. lit. "Prepared table." Code of *Torah* law, compiled by Joseph Caro (1488-1575). *Talmud* presents the broad discussion of the law, the background, while the *Shulchan Aruch* is a "prepared table," an orderly presentation of practical law and usage, regulating every aspect of the Jew's daily life and conduct.

Shulchan Aruch HaRav. The Code of Jewish Law compiled by Rabbi Schneur Zalman, the founder of *Chabad*, who was also known as The Rav. About 200 years after Rabbi Joseph Caro had published his master work, the *Shulchan Aruch*, Rabbi Schneur Zalman was asked to rewrite it to include the opinions, elucidations and decisions of generations of *Acharonim* in the interim period. The result is a masterpiece of clarity and authority.

Sitra Achra. "The other side," i.e. not the side of holiness; it is another term for "evil" in that it negates G-dliness. Anything that tends to separate from G-d belongs in the *sitra achra*, the root of evil.

Sod. See *Pardes*.

Succah. A hut or booth in which the Festival of Tabernacles, which occurs during the autumn, is observed.

Succot. Festival of Tabernacles, begins *Tishrei* 15.

Tallit. Prayer shawl worn by men during morning worship and during *Yom Kippur*.

Talmud. Post-Biblical Rabbinical literature, including *Mishnah* and later teachings, concluded around the sixth century of the Common Era.

Talmud chacham (pl. **talmidei chachamim**). Talmudic scholar(s) of high reputation.

Talmud Yerushalmi. *Talmud* compiled in Palestine, as distinct from the Babylonian Talmud. Both *Talmuds* follow the same pattern of *Mishnah* followed by *Gemarrah*. The authorities mentioned in the *Talmud Yerushalmi* all lived before c. 400 CE. The language used is Hebrew and Aramaic.

Talmudic. Relating to *Talmud*.

Talmudical. Relating to the *Talmud*.

Tanna (pl. **tannaim**). Derived from a word meaning "to teach" or "to repeat." The *Tannaim* taught their students to repeat and memorize the Law, since it was not recorded. The *Tannaim* were members of the Great Bet Din, and rendered decisions on religious and legal questions, usually, but not always, based upon their own interpretation of Scripture, after a vote was taken by all the participants in the *Bet Din* or Academy. The *Tannaim* and their disciples flourished from the time of Hillel and Shammai to that of Yehuda haNassi (a period of about two centuries). Their successors were the *Amoraim*. The period of the Tannaim, from 10-220 CE, is generally divided into five or six generations of scholars. Often generations overlap and a scholar was active in more than one period.

Tanya. Famous philosophical work by Rabbi Shneur Zalman of Liadi, in which the principles of *Chabad* are expounded. The name is derived from the initial word of this work (It has been taught). Also called *Likkutei Amarim*.

TAZ. Name by which David ben Samuel HaLevi (1586-1667) was known. Rabbi and *halachic* authority. The name is an acronym of one of his works *Turei Zahav*, a commentary on the four parts of the *Shulchan Aruch*.

Tefillin. Phylacteries worn by men during weekday morning worship; they contain verses from the Bible, including the *Shema*.

Teshuvah. Return; repentance.

Tiferet. lit. Beauty. Composition of first two emotion powers with kindness predominating.

Tishrei. A month in the Hebrew calendar; following Elul.

Torah. Used variously for *Chumash*, especially in scroll form, or for the entire body of Jewish religious Law (Bible, *Talmud*, *Midrash*, etc.)

Tosefta (pl. **Toseftot**). Means "addition" or "extension." The *Tosefta* is a collection of *Baraitot* (see *Baraita*) which states in complete form what the *Mishnah* often stated very concisely.

Tzaddik. Righteous man.

Tzedakah. Charity.

Tzitzit. Eight-string fringes worn by men in accordance

with commandment of Numbers 15:38; the four-cornered garment they are attached to.

Yesh. Something tangible.

Yetziat Mitzrayim. The exodus from Egypt.

Yetzirah. World of "Formation," third of the Four Worlds. See *Asiyah.*

Yom Kippur. Day of Atonement; *Tishrei* 10.

Zohar. Classic *Kabbalistic* work by Rabbi Shimon bar Yochai.

Contributors and biographical notes

YITZCHAK BLOCK
Ph.D. (Philosophy) Harvard University. Professor of Philosophy, University of Western Ontario. Leading North American authority on Aristotle. Noted scholar, writer and lecturer.

ZALMAN I. POSNER
Rabbi. Translator of several source works of Chabad literature. Brilliant exponent of mystical thought. Has lectured on all five continents. Author of *"Think Jewish."*

JONATHAN SACKS
M.A. (Philosophy) Cantab, Ph.D. (Philosophy) London. Rabbi. Principal, Jews' College; The Sir Immanuel Jakobovits Chair in Modern Jewish Thought, Jews' College, London, England.

J. IMMANUEL SCHOCHET
Ph.D. (Philosophy) University of Waterloo. Rabbi. Professor of Philosophy and Religion, Humber College, Toronto. Translator and lecturer. International authority on cults and comparative religion. Author of *"Mystical Concepts in Chassidism"* and other works.

ADIN STEINSALTZ

Rabbi, scholar and teacher. Head of the Israel Institute for Talmudic Publications, Jerusalem. The "Steinsaltz" Talmud is widely recognized as one of the major advances of Talmudic study of this century. Author of Talmudic and Mystical works including "The Essential Talmud" and "The Thirteen Petalled Rose."

Acknowledgements

Chabad Psychology and the Benoni of Tanya is reprinted from: Tradition, a Journal of Orthodox Jewish Thought, Vol. VI No. 1, Fall, 1963. Copyright 1963, The Rabbinical Council of America.

Anthropomorphism and Metaphors is reprinted from Mystical Concepts in Chassidism by J. Immanuel Schochet, published by Kehot Publication Society, New York, U.S.A.

Special thanks are due to:

Rabbi N. Sudak and Rabbi S.F. Vogel, London, England, and to Rabbi Y. Friedman, New York, U.S.A. for their guidance and assistance in the compilation of this volume, and to Mr. S.F. Hager for his assistance in checking source notes and references.

Compiled and Edited by Benzion and Hinda Rader.

NOTE

The traditional way of writing G-d's name (with a dash) has been used throughout this publication. The sources of this tradition are to be found in the Shulchan Aruch, Yoreh Deah, chapters 179 and 276 and commentaries; The Rav's Shulchan Aruch, Orach Chaim, chapter 85, par. 3.